THE HALLS OF ILLUSION

Shanon Hayes
The Halls of Illusion

All rights reserved
Copyright © 2024 by Shanon Hayes

—

Published by - Spines
ISBN: 979-8-89691-542-3

THE HALLS OF ILLUSION

THE TRUE STORY OF HOW GOD AND ONE WOMAN BEAT THE ILLUMINATI AND THE DEVIL AT THEIR OWN GAME

SHANON HAYES

I dedicate this book to the ones who did not make it: Myron May, Everston Brown, Keenan Anderson, Gavin Long, Alex Alexis. And to the woman who gave me the motivation Harriet Tubman. Also I dedicate this to the women who pushed me to write my truth Kimberly Phung.

CONTENTS

INTRODUCTION

Planet earth is a strange, magnificent and mysterious place. The galaxy is full of unknown anomalies we could never imagine. It is also full of conspiracy theories that are told in manner to make us believe certain stories in the world to be mere myths. Instead of the factual truths they are. I have never been a person who believes in such unorthodox topics. The few people I have come across over the years that would speak of these conspiracies as truth would concern me. I would simply think either they had a mental illness or stuck in their own delusional bubble. Reptilians running the world in secret, aliens, ghosts, secret societies and such were utterly ridiculous to me. I never had taken the time to step back and look at the world from a different perspective. I was told what I was told about how to see the world growing up and I went with this programming. My life experiences have most definitely changed my mind about these conspiracies to being not just myths and fantasy to full blown reality. I decided to write this book to Glorify the Most High and bring awareness to the false narrative being portrayed upon the masses. This is a worldwide phenomenon happening to innocent people and no one's doing anything about it. Even with the hundreds of thousands of reports being placed about these unfathomable crimes against humanity. This unheard-of crime is called gang stalking, targeted individuals and community cause stalking. This rabbit hole is hidden in plan sight. The Governments of this world are behind the scenes playing invisible puppet masters in our unsuspecting lives. This is a one-sided game that is played using real people as their pawns.

The reptilian draconian species are in fact a real-life nightmare. They are these secret societies of elites and unelected rulers who have been plotting and planning against humanity to infiltrate and dominate the world with the evil forces they conger and make blood sacrifices to. They also kidnap our children to torture and harvest adrenochrome from their brain. To ensure they can remain young and have a life force. I know this sounds far out and like a movie, but it is true. The Freemasons and Illuminati hire paid actors that follow victims where they go while performing organized routines of collaborated chaos to create inconveniences. This is known as street theatre. Claims of nonconsensual surgical implants installed into the intended targets bodies. This allows the gang stalkers to track, monitor and control the actions of the victim. They use directed microwave weapons that the gang stalkers install in different areas of the victim's home or through the walls next door. They can also point them in the target's direction through the walls of neighboring homes. They use technology to project sound and voices into the mind of the victim which is called voice to skull. This is done to create psychological torture. These victims call themselves targeted individuals or T.I 's for short. These people are in a mass torture program meant to slowly break them down. Gang stalking is an umbrella term describing a series of techniques used by a group to instill mental instability within a victim with the intent to discredit, sabotage, harass, and extort, even driving victims to unalive themselves. A victim of gang stalking can have a reputation, credibility, relationships, career and entire lives put into ruins. Techniques such as mind games, perception, manipulation, organized gang stalking covert harassment, constant illegal surveillance and electronic harassments are used to push victims to mental instability. Proving one's targeted torture can be very challenging. There is near to no help coming from any law enforcement agencies. This allows the program to be extremely effective.

The government pays family members to turn their backs on the targeted family member to ensure the harassment can be done without the victim receiving any help. Isolation and no support make the torture tactics to be more effective. MKULTRA is another horrific program that is intended for the victims to seem delusional or unstable. The problem with this scenario is it is medically impossible for two different individuals to share the same delusion. These incidents are being reported all around the world daily. Directed energy weapons technology uses sound beams, particle beams, microwave beams using these methods to control will create a on demand psychotic episode. Voice to scull can cause a victim to hear audio inside their own head completely inaudible to anyone else. Also, remote neurol monitoring is a form of monitoring functioning nero images. This is a way of accessing a person's coding thoughts without a person's knowledge, or consent. It is also a form of synthetic telepathy in which brains can communicate with each other just by thinking, which is achieved through an intermediary such as a computer. These incidents of involuntary Guinee pigs are being implemented all over the world. Through this program their goal is to achieve the targeted individual to become irrational and walk themselves to their own death. Let's discuss what organizations are behind this program. Government agencies, law enforcement, C.I.A., F.B.I, pharmaceutical companies, secret societies, criminal organizations are just a few examples of gang stalking.

Then there is a certain category called the chosen ones. Chosen ones are chosen by God to follow our spiritual path and answer the call. I believe I am one of the chosen ones. I was faced with certain challenges brought on by demonic forces. These challenges then had to be overcome while remaining on our spiritual path during the entire experience. We must protect our unique spiritual gifts. These demonic entities enter our lives in the forms of people, friends and loved ones. It also involves negative energy projection, black magic, hexes, curses, and spiritual assassination. Please do your own research on these topics to become well informed on your own terms. We must all go on our own journey to enlightenment. Use my story as a steppingstone to gain momentum in the right direction for your own wisdom.

In February 2020, I began having experiences that changed me and my entire world. I now see the world through an entirely different lens which I call the lens of truth. I used to be like most of you, until my entire world was turned upside down. I began school in Modesto CA. at Western Pacific Trucking School. I had taken a year to get the funding all put together and to get the proper paperwork done to attain free funding for my education. I was excited to start school so that I could finally have financial freedom and stability in a career that would be fulfilling. I had plans to buy a home and finally begin a life I could be proud of. The night before I was to start school I received a call from my grandmother Marylin. She called me up and made the oddest statement to me. She blatantly stated, "Don't go to school". I was confused why someone I loved so much would try to get me to not do something that would better my life. I thought she was going to give me some words of encouragement and instead I got discouragement. Then my father tells me " Shanon , why are you going to school it is going to be waste of your time". Now two of my family members had tried to disway me from something positive so I immediately contacted my counselor from the county. I shared with her the discussions I had just had, and she was shocked. She said to ignore them and quickly reminded me I was doing the right thing. She then gave me some positive words of motivation before hanging up the phone. I went to bed early to be bright, and bushy tailed for my first day.

I attended the four-week program and gained my permit for Commercial Truck Driving License. I pushed myself and tested and passed for my triples and doubles and my tankers endorsements. While I attended this school, I was assigned an instructor. This instructor was very unprofessional and would sexually harass me daily. He would stand in front of me holding his clip board and announce to me that "you know people are going to hire you by what I write about you"! He was abusing his authority, and I was made to feel uncomfortable and knew if I was to not allow his abuse, I was not going to get a job I was so thrilled to be working towards. I almost quit two weeks in due to this harassment. I felt like if I quit, I was giving up on myself. I couldn't let this creepy immature man stop me from doing what I had intended to complete. The week of graduation the school had made me an appointment with the D.M.V. to perform the pretrip and the driving skills tests using the diesel owned by the school. A few days before my appointment was when Covid 19 hit and the entire world shut down. This included the D.M.V. which meant I was unable to complete my commercial driving license. I was devasted that I had yet again put my heart into something that did not work out. A few months later I decided to contact a sexual harassment attorney to file a lawsuit against the trucking school for the crime committed against me while attending. I knew other women would be coming through this school and this instructor was going to keep up his behavior if it was not brought to the light. I had attended a two-year criminal justice associates college program previous years and had multiple male instructors who never made me feel they were being inappropriate towards me in any way.

Life had changed for the entire world, and everything would be shut down. I was being pressured by my father to pay my rent and began to think outside the box to make money for survival.

I lived in Twain Harte, California, at this time, and my backyard was the Stanislaus National Forest. So, as you can assume, there are lots of campers in the area. I began to see bright lights floating back and forth across the mountain from me. I grabbed my flashlight and shined it back in their direction. I made waving designs and such to let them know I was aware of their presence. It was kind of fun, like a game. I was thinking that it was people camping and playing around with me. While camping outside across the way from me. I assumed some campers had a bright light on a drone or something. I was outside a lot, and it happened every night when I was relaxing on the porch. Also, I was hearing many different bird calls at night. Birds that were not ever part of the natural and usual sounds from the forest. The birds were very loud, and it would go on every night as well. I had started to notice that planes and drones were constantly flying around my area, which was way out of the norm. These strange things had been occurring, and it definitely drew me with curiosity.

The world had shut down, and I had bills to pay. I was still in contact with an ex of mine and was venting my concerns with him as to how or what I was going to do to accomplish this. He made a bold statement to me. That piqued my interest, which was, "Why don't you go share your skills with the world?" I said, "Skills, what skills?". He said, "You know you were born to fuck. That's. That's what you were made for"! I was thrown off by his rough and jagged wording of who he proclaimed me to be. I sat on his suggestion for a few weeks and then began doing some research on what websites to go to that were made for a woman of my age. Being that I was 43 at the time, I was not trying to come off as something I wasn't, and that was young. I found a website called List Crawler, which had a category for M.I.L.F. s for women 40 and over. L.O.L. I pondered on a sexy, catchy name that would draw the men in and decided to use Horny Holly. I had come up with that name when I was 19 years old, just being silly. If it was the time to use such a name, this was the time. I then took some hot pics of myself creating a profile. It was official. I only was thinking I was going to make a lot of men happy in the world. I had only good intentions when I put myself out there like that.

I became very popular very fast. I had so many text messages it was hard to keep up. But I answered every single one with my two own little fingers. I knew that in the line of work I had chosen to enter, I would be coming across some odd characters out in the world. And by gosh, that's exactly what happened. I received a text message in my first week ,that I was tracked by G.P.S. in my car, my phone was hacked, and they could hear everything I said in my car. I brushed off the message but kept it in the back of my mind in case I would need it in the future. I thought to myself, "self-people are weirdos out there!". I also met a man on the phone who proclaimed to be C.I.A. and was also a captain of a fishing boat company who invited me to Hawaii, but I never met up with him in the years we spoke on the phone. Then, the next week, I was on a phone call with a man who asked me if I had a baby or if I knew of someone who had a baby in my line of work that would let him ejaculate on the baby. And started to tell me the story of how he found a hooker the week prior allowed him to do just that on her 2-month-old baby. I immediately hung up the phone in utter rage and shock at the request of this sick, demented man. Right when I hung up the phone with this man, I contacted the ex-C.I.A. agent man I had previously met on the phone as well. I alerted him as to my discovery of this disturbed individual. His reply was, "how can we find him if you were talking on an online app?" I agreed and left the conversation feeling defeated by the evil I knew I came face to face with.

The first 8 months I was in business for myself, I found when I transferred to a new phone that I had 30,000 texts messages that I replied to personally, never ever a group text. EVER.... I held myself to a high standard even though I was an escort. I was the kind of a classy lady that would come knock on your door in a raincoat and high heels to open it up wide to reveal my sexy silky or lace lingerie laying upon my milky white skin with my hair done up and glossy, plump lips to kiss. That's how I ran my show. I was never a street hooker, a low-class dumpster drug addict. I was doing nothing but sharing my love and making smiles. I was completely unaware of the true distorted evil lying in wait for me underneath the surface. I began to tell my family little white lies as to my whereabouts when I would go meet my clients for three days in

Modesto, Ca., I thought the entire time I was covering my butt only to find out that they all knew about my promiscuous adventures I had been partaking in. I had decided to make my reservations at a nice hotel I knew of from my youth. It had an indoor spa and ,just had a good vibe, as I remembered. The rooms also had two entrances, one that made sure my clients didn't have to show I.D. and gave more privacy to them. I thought it was a nice thing for me to do at the time. I also was able to get a rewards card with this hotel, which added up, and I ended up having a lot of free nights after I realized I had this benefit. I would set up my rendezvous weeks in advance with my clients and began to have a solid list of clients I could depend on to show up when scheduled. It was a great choice in the beginning, but I soon came to see that things were not on point with this Hotel line. I became acquaintances with the security guard at the hotel and had my own private security, it felt like. He would let me in the spa any time I wanted, day

or night. He also alerted me to other guests talking and gossiping about me, saying that I was a bop! A bop? I was not sure exactly what that meant and was angered by the fact I had strangers I didn't even know putting my name in their mouths.

One of the days I checked into The Clarion Hotel, I was given a room that was very accommodating and comfortable, except for a brown cardboard box that was attached and painted to the wall. When I told the Hotel about this oddity and my concerns about how the box on the wall was constantly making baby birds chirp loudly, causing lots of noise. When I complained about this situation, I was told it was baby birds that fell in the wall from the outside of the building, but that didn't even make sense to me at all. I love animals deeply and couldn't imagine hurting cute little birds, so I just dealt with the annoyance. It began every time I came to the hotel, and I was given this same room. I knew this was not normal and made no sense, so I made a video of these weird incidents. To cover my butt. They also had not fixed the leaking air conditioner that would drip on the Berber carpet. The constant dripping would soak the floor completely, even if I put towels under the drip. This caused the room to smell musty. After this experience, I was fed up with the treatment at this hotel. I then decided to entertain my clients at other Hotels in the area. I also started gathering clients in San Francisco and had leveled up from Modesto. I am glad I made the video because it let me know that my intuition is on point, and I never realized that experience would circle around four years later because it shows the true intentions of the Illuminati and how they were trying to drive me into the hole they ultimately dug for themselves. Not to mention the fact I almost committed suicide four times during this season of my life due to the outrageous scenarios being created for me. One client I had met would show and treat me very disrespectfully. I did not like him and sometimes would not answer his phone calls. One time we met up, and he had said," I want to introduce you to the Grove. It's a group of business men, they want to meet you". I did not know who the Grove was and was not impressed like he thought I would be. I blew off his comment and never asked him about it. Eventually, I stopped seeing him because I just felt like something was off with this man. I still had not been aware at this time that people were plotting on me, so I did not even take the time to Google the Grove until I met another man later.

God was right there for me the entire time, guiding me to the knowledge I needed to survive. I strived every day to live, knowing there were other people out in this world that this devilish cult was hurting. I would picture other innocent people they were harming and could only imagine how scared they all were. I knew that this was happening to not only to me but to a lot of other people. They come after the weak and prey on their pain. I had one thing to prove, and that was God is real, and your all going to see. They never thought that He was going to step in. God was always reminding me of the mental and physical strength I held inside. I had to get justice, and I had to keep going for this one reason. I just pictured a weak, scared, confused individual on the side of the road being bombarded by this illusion of hate, and that made me mad. I had to live and survive for all of the ones out there who couldn't speak out or were dying. Getting to this point to share these atrocities with you as the reader and the whole world is an ultimate victory. The Most High called upon me, and I answered the call with no hesitation. My story needed to be shared to help raise the vibration to help bring The Kingdom of God to this earth. As above, so below. The world is being reset and balanced as I write these words down, and new beginnings are upon us all. The masses are going to wake up to the breakdown of the matrix and no longer see the world through rose-colored glasses without distorted truths. Behind every word I have written is my truth and nothing but my truth. I finally feel-good saying that without someone telling me to be quiet or, worse, shut the F… up! I was with my babies daddy, who was very abusive for 11 years, and he never told me to shut the f up, so for strangers I met for the entire year I would talk about anything would tell me to shut the f up. That was out for me. The more people kept telling me to shut the f up it only made me talk louder and more.

The first months of escorting it were exciting for me. For the simple fact that I was financially independent for the first time in my life. The gentleman I had come across had me feeling very confident about myself and my life. I had acquired a pretty good, dependable list of clients and a steady flow of money. The clients I met were all very kind to me, but one. He was phantasmagoric and requested very cruel and unusual fetishes of me. He was tall, dark and handsome. He was very fit and had an exquisite body. His eyes were blue as the ocean was deep and drew me in every time we met. He asked me to do something called a hard 40, which I had no clue what that meant I agreed to the request. It really wasn't until the day he walked into my room with a bag of tricks. Inside the bag, he had a belt that was very thick leather, and it looked like it had been used many times before. He spoke to me about the acts we were about to perform in a manner as if it was a ritual with how we would count out the strong, hard lashes of the bell against my bare. And not the last 10 I would be allowed to count out at my own pace. He also stated that at the end of it all, he wanted to see one single tear trickle down my face so he could wipe it away for me. I took his assault like a champ, and not one tear fell until the next day when I was black and blue from belt marks across my bottom. I had other clients coming those three days who saw my bruises and were appalled that I let someone do such things to me. I sat on a pillow the next day and cried in pain and tried healing my wounds as best I could. He then wanted me to vomit on his penis when I would give him blow jobs which I thought was disgusting. The last request he had of me was to feed him his feces by sticking my finger in his anus. This was the last time I ever saw him again. When the abuse I was to endure at the hands of this man over the next few years was beyond physical. He was trying to affect my self-esteem and my worth. He would constantly up the ante on his rough games and then demand I take less money for my services, which I would refuse to lower my standards too. This man was just the first of many who began to enter my life at a slow, steady pace, bringing me nothing but drama and trying to make me feel less then.

I started to call this event The Dark Carnival. This was not just my own community; people coming from a lot of other places came to town to obliterate my entire being. The entire town was constantly full of cars honking and shining bright lights at me. An entire community was trying to destroy the persona and job I had created. As well as to drive me crazy. I knew I could not tell anyone what was going on because that was the point of what they were doing. They wanted me to tell someone like a therapist or the cops in order for me to be put away. I did not even thinking back to how I previously heard my father telling my son about some kind of money being put in an offshore account. As far as I have known about, my family's financial status was regular middle class. We were not of the upper Esh elance consanguinity. Not by any means in need of offshore accounts. I do know from personal experience that money will make people do peculiar things. But I did not realize they had stolen anything from me at this time, and why would I? They were my family. Who would ever think in the form of such betrayal? I knew something outlandish was happening when I went into Turlock; it had a different vibe, and the entire town was chock-a-block. What caught my attention the most and alerted me that things were diffidently out of sorts was when I needed to wash my car. I like to wash my car by hand so I would pick a stall at any of the open car washes available. Any time of the day, they would be wall to wall with mobs of loud cars revving their engines along with blaring music. There are a large number of individuals standing around as if it were the place to be. Almost like one big party was running all over Turlock from end to end. The amount of trash and garbage being deposited into the trash cans was unbelievable as well. The car wash attendants or owners could not keep up with the constant bombardment being placed on them. Trash was constantly bursting onto the ground and the parking lots and left wafting in the wind. There were also multiple interlopers who all seemed to know who I was and were calling out my name. It really freaked me out because I didn't understand how all these people knew who I was. I was just a regular girl from central California. I was clueless as to the extent of what truly was lurking in my presence and constantly surrounding my personal space. I almost felt famous. Not the kind of fame that I was wanting. My Spidey senses were up, and I instinctively knew this was inferior to what God wanted me to be known for in this world. It was better than being treated like a mere sex object or play toy. This cult simply didn't recognize my A.K.A persona. Horny Holly was not me. I may have been doing somethings that was not up to moral codes in God's eyes, but I was never doing anything to be malicious or to cause harm. I was only trying to make some men smile and maybe be in a happier place with my sincere touch and my love. I have never robbed anyone or tried to trick them out of a session for their money. I may not have chosen the right way to go about my financial problems during COVID-19, but I can stand before you all today with an honest heart and true repentance for my admitted wrongs. Knowing that these experiences and choices made me who I am today. I had to learn these lessons,, and it had to be through my own ignorance that I did not see my true worth during this time. This was God's plan before I was even born. God had made a way for the veil to be lifted from my eyes so I could choose to change or not. He gave me the choice, and that's our free will, which he so lovingly gives us. I was either going to learn or ignore the signs and synchroneities he had to show me. If I had decided not to see the truth and continue to live the lifestyle I was partaking in, it would have been my own demise. Seeing people and situations for what they really were and not for the false hooded lies or delusions they wanted me to see. This was a false persona I had created for myself out of necessity, but it was not who I truly am in the spirit. I am Shannon, and most importantly, a child of the Most High God. This is where this group went wrong. They took God out of the equation completely. God, being the lions, shares and crucial pieces of me and my internal puzzle that they all missed. No one even took into account that I might have a strong bond and verifiable relationship with God. Not one person in the community or society ever took the time to get to know the authentic me. Not my friends or my family. Talk about dropping the ball. You would think that when discussing a person to sacrifice, you would want to know this major veritably in the sacrificial victims' beliefs.

I began to be braided with false phone calls, text messages and voicemails. Being they were fake or unintentional was how to create wasted time and money for me. This cult was paying a multitude of commoners to contact me. Directing them to get close to me to ensure information would be told to them straight from the horse's mouth. I was pretty good at telling my business to others freely and openly. The Illuminati had turned my personal life into a board game for their own demented pleasure. Not to mention how my regular clients, whom I usually could depend on, had become very unreliable and letting me down by not showing up or constantly negotiating my rate. New clients I had been contacted by simply did not ever have any aspirations to follow through. As I stated previously, money will make people do peculiar things. It was a constant stream of letdowns and pulling the rug out from under me. They really thought this childish, immature behavior was entertaining. These strangers and community members were constantly laughing and snickering at me everywhere I went. They most definitely were having the time of their lives, as far as I could tell. The best part of it for these creatures was how I was completely and utterly oblivious to what they were constantly up to. The twisted plans to create daily strife and problems for me were hard to bear. I had to be my own cheerleader for many repeated days just to get up in the morning. Knowing I had to endure in my silence trauma with no one to turn to but my best friend, God. I did it over and over again. The continuous blockages and countless obstacles that were placed on my figurative and literal me were seemingly an ocean of pain with a life raft or land in sight.

The Freemasons had no problems in their conquest against ruining me. It was as easy as a phone call and a bank transfer of payment to whomever they needed on any day, with their endless willing and able-bodied friends and cult members who were more than happy to oblige anything requested. They had the police stations in their pockets, courts, restaurants, hotels and stores. It did not matter. If I traverse that business or whatever is,maybe you better believe they had someone to fulfill this quota of torture upon me. This hateful cult was purposefully creating pain and confusion for me in hopes I would simply grow distressed to the point and I no longer wanted to live anymore. It was crazy how it was happening right before my eyes and under my nose, and I could not see it. I could not imagine in my lifetime the extent of hate that was being directed towards me done with smiling faces. It's like meeting someone, and you go to shake their hand with your right hand, but behind your back, in your left hand, you have a knife waiting to jam it straight in their back. I was experiencing these difficult situations daily and didn't catch on for a very, very long time. I cried a lot when I was alone and would talk to God about my sadness. I went to God for everything, as we all should! He has always been there for me when no one was, and this was a time when I really needed his comfort and direction more than I had ever needed him before. I spurned and would not allow these psychotic individuals to dismantle my life or the lives of others who were being harmed. When I did realize the awe-inspiring conspiracy against my life, I was bound and determined to figure out what was happening to me because I had watched too many episodes of X-Files and Unsolved Mysteries to not be interested in the oddities that began occurring and the horrific unwarranted harassment being done to me.

Another client I came across was very charismatic, and we had a lot in common, mostly music. We began to talk on the phone for hours and hours in the weeks between my next trip down to Modesto. His name was Maui, and he was from Maui. He was short, not attractive, and had a scratchy voice. He was very outgoing and reminded me of Steveo from Jack Ass off M.T.V. I really liked his personality and overlooked he wasn't really my type. He then began to ask me over to this house for dinner, and we became close. He never judged me for my profession and was cool with me making appointments on our calls for new clients, which gave me a chance to make more money. I was spreading myself very thin and making so much money in the process. I was driven like the winter snow. I would pass out from exhaustion on his California king bed often. Then, he would always take pictures of me sleeping. I thought it was cute at the time, but now I know about astral projection, and he was trying to astral project into my dreams. This is a way to plant thoughts and memories into my mind without me being aware. His parents had a bar b que, and I was invited to join them. I must say it was the strangest array of people. There were all kinds of different groups, and no one really matched in any manner. Punk rockers, hillbillies, hippies, old people, young people, and I didn't feel comfortable at all. His mother had a great set up of food and drinks, and it was a lovely and delicious bar b que. Maui's mother made a statement in front of the entire group of people that was meant to embarrass me, but I don't get embarrassed. She said, " Maui, this one is not our type; you like women tall and with long black hair." Being that I am only 5,5 and have mid length blonde hair, I knew it was a purposeful statement. I brushed off the incident and didn't mention this to him at all. Like a duck in water, it rolled off my back. The fake calls really amped up and were getting annoying to me, so I stopped doing our calls for a while. Looking back and knowing what I know now, this was the beginning of my spiritual assassination and trying to break my connection with the Most High. The rituals they go through have levels, and this was level one, destroying my self-esteem and trying to knock me out of my own comfort zone with myself. As I became more knowledgeable in myself and my research, I was being spiritually activated, and my protection from the spiritual realm was only becoming stronger and stronger unnoticed to this narcissistic satanic community. This was God's secret alert button. The warring angels I was calling upon heard me. Every time I was hurt and crying, I was sending out signals and silent messages in my prayers. He immediately put all my warring angels on point to come to earth to my rescue. I had no idea at the time how powerful my prayers were, but I sure do today. I will never forget what God has done for me. The amazing thing is I was blindfolded and put in an labyrinth. I found my way out blindfolded with no information than what God was telling me and guiding me to do. They wanted to put in an oubliette. I am truly a walking miracle. Time went by and I was spending more and more time at Maui's house and less time at my father's house. Even though I was up on my rent and bills I was not interested in staying at his home. I never told any of my grown children where I was staying in Modesto. So, the day my daughter came knocking on Mauis door was very odd. Hannah showed up out of the blue one afternoon. I asked her how she knew where I was and how she found his address. She said she got on People Finder, but I didn't even know Maui's government name so how would she? I dismissed this incident and was just glad to see my daughter's beautiful face at the door. We had a great visit, and I shared with her how I was going to give her my little Tahoe truck because I had bought a Camry. I was so excited to be able to help her out in a manner I never thought I would be able to.

This same week I received a random phone call from my son Austin saying," Grandpa said he's putting your stuff out in the street because you haven't paid the rent for your room". I couldn't believe what I was hearing because I knew I had paid my rent in full. My intuition even told me to take pictures of the money and have my father sign a rental. I felt something in the air was evolving. I knew it had to do with the conversation I had with him about sexual acts I had heard he did with Austin and Hannah. I just knew it. I took the pictures to show my grandmother because she was the one who owned the house. I felt, for some reason, I was going to have to defend myself from him, and I did have to show her this proof. But when I discussed this matter about his lies, she didn't care. She didn't believe me. When Austin sent this message about my things on the road, I went immediately to ask Maui if he would borrow his dad's truck to retrieve my things from the streets before people plundered my items. We went to Twain Harte that afternoon, and sure thing, all my things were boxed and had been put in garbage bagged out in the road. It was also kind of overcast and was threatening to rain. This was the beginning of the war against me, projected by my family. I quietly gathered up my things and moved into Maui's home.

My living situation was not ideal because I didn't want to live with a man, especially in such a short time of knowing him. Maui and I were getting along fabulously, and he even introduced me to a few of his friends who had come to town. His friend was a Hollywood stuntman. His friend and his finds girlfriend had just come from a nudist colony in Stockton. It was the same one that Cary Stanier, the Yosemite serial killer and his brother the kidnapped child Steven Stainer. Cary was arrested at this same nudist colony. Now that I know about this cult and the mass reach it has, I now know that they all knew each other and were connected. So creepy, right? Looking back, I am so glad I did not mention any of these things that were happening to me to Maui or anyone. I just quietly started to go inside myself. The people around me didn't want to accept me, and I had to accept myself, which led me to be able to go internally and start talking to the divine in my life. Even though I was not living a righteous life, I always knew I could go to him I grew in my knowledge of the occult, I had no clue my family was involved. I now look at what I am writing and connect so many dots today that make sense to me. It's crazy how a few years of gang stalking and going through all these supernatural experiences I had been through had led me down many rabbit holes during my research. These rabbits holes can quickly twerk your perception of how life truly is and bring you to a new level of consciousness. I began to learn how far the government and cults will go to destroy one person. Living under this controlled environment all my life and not realizing it till my late 40s.

The living situation with Maui was going great,, and I thought, we were falling in love with each other. I was shocked when, just like a light switch, one day, he was for me, then the very next day, he asked me to move my things into his guest room. He stated we could be friends or roommates,, and that was the end of our relationship. So, I did just that. In the meantime, I was looking for other options and places to move to because he was so ruthless. He would shut his bedroom door and have very loud conversations with other women that he said were his type. He was also bringing other escorts over to the house right in front of me. He made comments like, "you're never going to be able to move out, and you're not going anywhere." He also introduced me to a tattoo artist that had started a large tattoo on my shoulder and then never returned any of my calls to set up the final appointment to finish the 700.00 tattoo he had started. The way Maui broke it off with me was very off for me because I was always the one who broke up with men. I never got dumped, especially by someone that I had felt sorry for in the beginning. I suppose this scenario was created to make me feel some type of way. This whole ugly scene made me say W.T.F., Knowing that whatever Maui was doing to me had nothing to do with me or how I felt about myself. I have always been confident and known who I am to the core.

One huge experience that showed me how much I am loved and appreciated by others was when I was hit by my husband with a hairdryer, which was an incident that landed me in the California prison system. Multiple women would come to me for advice or prayer and always gave me the utmost respect. These experiences gave me the confidence in myself to be who I really am without any holding back or trying to fit in with the so-called crowd. God had come into my life and changed me from the inside out. The Highest had taken all this trauma and bad experiences from my childhood, and helped heal them. God came into my life to save me from this cult. I am probably the only person you will hear say that they are happy they went to prison. If I had not gone to prison, I know for a fact that I would be dead on the ground, just like these people wanted. This is a fact. The Lord saved my life, bottom line. He woke me up with His promises. When I was put in this prison alone ,my friends and family abandoned me while there. He showed me I was not alone, and he opened his arms to me. When they all turned their backs and abandoned me. Be still and know I am God. While being incarcerated, you can either choose not to learn from the experience, or you can grow in the Lord and gain knowledge that will empower you to be the person you are meant to be. I was able to find my purpose through pain. I took every opportunity to change to ensure I would not come back to such a place. If God did not save me, I would not be here to share my testimony of this tale that I am unfolding for you in the pages of this book.

CHAPTER 1

THE JERRY SPRINGER EPISODE

I want to give you about some insight into my prison trip. Well, it goes a little something like this. In 2007, I was working in a local grocery store in the bakery/deli department, where I met a customer named Daniel Melton. He had a 10-year-old daughter named Mandy and a 15-year-old son named Brandon, who was going to school with my oldest daughter, Tawnie. He also said he was a homeowner and had a nanny. I thought he really had his life together. We had gone out for a few months when he said he loved me and wanted to marry me. He was not concerned that I had 3 children of my own Tawnie 15, Hannah 13, and my son Austin 11. I had been raised as a single parent most of their lives due to their father, J. Roy, always being incarcerated for robbery and drugs. We had a very volatile relationship, and I suffered massive abuse for 11 years. He accepted this part of my life. Which a lot of men did not want to be a part of. I felt for his 10-year-old daughter, Mandy, because I was led to believe she did not have a mother. This was where I went wrong because I took the easy route for the first time in my life. I had never been married in my life and wanted that love and stability. I was not thinking spiritually at all about my decision because I did not even know who God was at that time. I thought I was my own God at this point. While growing up, my grandmother was the only adult that I looked up to, and she was a complete and total atheist. I had no spiritual direction while I was growing up. When I was raising the kids, I would think my bills were paid, the kids had clothes for school and were in sports, and we always had a roof over our heads always. I would sit back and think, man, I'm good! I did all this by myself. But today, I know, no, I had nothing today with what was taken care of during these times. It was always God.

Daniel not only made me believe his love for me was real but also that he would be good to my three children. I was just at the end of graduating San Joaquin Valley College for Criminal Justice in Modesto, CA. I had attended The Stanislaus County Sheriff's Department Police Academy. I even ran 8 miles to pass the physical aspect of the academy. I had been attending my studies in criminal justice for 2 years and drove round trip 3 hours just to try to better myself and the lives of my children. I truly wanted to be a part of law enforcement to help victims and the innocent in the world. I had been done so wrong by the justice system growing up I thought I could make a difference in the world. I was going to start out as a correctional officer, as there was a prison in my area called Sierra Conservation Center in Jamestown. I had dated the sergeant years before and knew this was a great, secure job to have. I suppose I let my mind take over and not my heart. He asked me to marry him, and I accepted. When I accepted his proposal, he required that I not follow through with my dream in law enforcement. He said he would take care of me and the kids. He even made statements he did not want me around all those men I would encounter if I entered this career.

My marriage led me into an entire cast of characters and actors from a Jerry Springer episode. When Daniel had said he had a nanny, I thought great if we could use one with our band of children, we had together. 8 months into my marriage, I found out that the nanny was not the nanny at all. Daniel had been arrested for marijuana, and on our way to the jail to bail him out, she looked back at me while she was driving. She had told straight out she was not a nanny, and she was, in fact, Mandy's mother and Daniels wife. I knew something was not right the night before I married him. God was trying to tell me not to do it. I tried to break it off that night before, but he begged and pleaded with me. I ignored this warning, and I ended up giving in to his cries and we got married the next morning at The Sands Hotel in Reno. The ceremony was small, and it only included him, me and his daughter Mandy. My own children did not want anything to do with it, and they did not attend the wedding. This should have been a red flag for me, but for some reason, I couldn't see the danger I was entering blindly.

My intuition tried to stop me the night of the wedding. I told him I did not want to marry him, and he freaked out. He begged and cried all night until I eventually gave in. I didn't know that the Holy Spirit was warning me because I didn't know about God or spirituality. Ignoring my intuition was either the biggest mistake or the biggest blessing because it eventually did lead me straight to God. Either way, after going to prison and all I endured from my false marriage, I never ignored my gut feeling. I stand before you a person working on my healing daily with God. He is guiding me to my purpose and the life He intended for me. All three of my children did not like Daniel from the gate. Due to Daniels's son, Brandon, had written a hit list of fellow students that was found in his locker at school. This had happened a few years previously to me meeting Daniel. Tawnie, my oldest daughter, had been placed on Brandon's murder list as number 26. Her best friend Raquel was number 3, and I had to ask Raquel, 'What in the heck did you do to him, girl? He had it out for you'! I would stand up for Daniel by telling my children, "You all can't judge Daniel by what Brandon did." But I see now that Brandon was crazy because his father, Daniel was a straight, violent, narcissistic, scary psychopath. There is a saying "The fruit doesn't fall far from the tree". (Quote) I was not thinking with the spirit and had no excuse. The enemy sure knew what he was doing. He was smiling as he was attempting to lead me to the Lake of Fire along with him. The enemy was more than happy to help me with distractions and chaos. Then, using my empathy against me. I was unaware of Lucifer's true presence and did not pay attention to all the warning signs the spirit world and my ancestors were trying to get to me.

I never ignore the Highest God, Spirit, angels and ancestors today. They all have saved me many times from the traps and snares of these Satanic killers. They planned and plotted against me but never could fulfilltheir evil schemes. For example, God would simply propose to shut my phone off and lay low, go into hermit mode. Sometimes, I would recognize this when it was happening, and other times, I wouldn't even know until later how blessed and lucky I was. The Most High saved over and over again. To this day ,I don't even know the extent. He was always working in the background. He never left me.

During my marriage, it was full verbal and physical abuse. I had entered a marriage with a Karmic. A wicked, evil man I thought I could change or help. He had been diagnosed with a mental disorder called intermediate rage disorder that he would fuel with vats of vodka down his throat daily. These escapades would only exasperate his already sketchy rage condition. He was even put on lithium, which made him act like a zombie. I am not saying I was perfect. It takes to. I take the blame for my part as well. Alcohol was a major common denominator in my marriage. We used to drink together a lot. Which eventually did lead me into full blown alcoholism. We would drink, fight, and rage, until blacking out. Waking up the next day sore and beaten up. Black and blue bruises from head to toe. Along with the most popular punch in the woman beaters club. The famous, fat, purple black eye. I was always wearing big, giant sunglasses to cover up my abuse. I once had to quit my job at Save Mart Grocery store because he beat me up so bad I was ashamed to go to work. I couldn't allow her to see what he had done to me. My only thought was to up and quit. We would constantly get into physical battles and verbal assaults. We eventually decided to go to see a marriage counselor. During these sessions at the therapist's office, we both were leaving out the fact we were drinking to the extent we were. The therapist then asked me if I would want to try some medication to help me get my chemical balance together. He had put me on five medications. He put me on Seroquel, Depakote, Trazadone, Prozac and Clonazepam. On top of these medications, I was taking. These were 5 hardcore medications I did not think I would have to look up. I was unaware that I should be concerned for my life from my licensed doctor and therapist. I trusted these so-called professionals, as well as the medical Dr who validated his prescriptions. These, put together, can cause life-threatening side effects. Something never brought to my attention not once. I was gaining so much weight from the side effects as well. I gained 120 lbs. during this year, and ½ I took this death concoction. I had even made an appointment for my son Austin to speak with Dr. Rourke. I was truly concerned for my son's mental health. I was not allowed in during his session. After the session was over, I asked Dr. Rouke what he could share with me. He only mentioned that my son had lucid dreams. Austin only agreed to go that one time for me, but I was just glad I could get him to go at all.

Even though we had been supposedly working on our marriage. Daniel and I continued to fight over everything, but mostly about the past betrayals. I could not seem to let go. His wife being the nanny was a blockage in my heart I could not release at this time. Holding on to what he had done to me was only making me sick. That's the parasitic mind set.

Their mission and assignment is to perpetuate this unproductive energy to keep you from finding your purpose. They love to keep you in a cycle of trauma and anger. I was lost in the spells and tricks this group was doing over me to prevent me from seeing what had been really going on. Redirecting my path right under my nose.

Even though I had done all the paperwork to get them divorced and made her move out about 3 weeks after learning the truth. I just couldn't get over these betrayals. I decided to forgive him. I then remarried him in a ceremony at the Tuolumne County courthouse, with no one there but a clerk as our witness. I did not want to see the truth, and I should have left him when I found out she was still, in fact, his wife and not the nanny. We fought over that a lot. I was going to leave him soon after finding out, but he pulled a knife out and stabbed himself right in the neck when I told him I was leaving him. When he stabbed himself, I screamed for my oldest daughter, Tawnie, who was in her room down the hall from ours. She quickly came running to my pleas for help. Tawnie came in with superhuman strength and pushed him out of the way, grabbed my arm, and shielded me from him as I ran out the bedroom door. As we were pulling out of the driveway, Daniel came running after the car with blood pouring out of him and rubbing it all over my car door. Tawnie and I then drove up to my friend John's house, whom I had known for over 13 years, who lived up the hill in Mi-Wuk in search of a place of safety. John was always a homebody and did not like to leave the mountain ever, but Tawnie and I talked him into coming with us down to Sonora to eat at Taco Bell. After leaving Taco Bell, we began to head back up the hill, but suddenly, I got pulled over by the Sonora Police Department. They approached the driver's side window ,asked all three of us to exit the vehicle, and sat us down on the curb. They began to conduct an investigation as to the stabbing of my husband. Daniel had smeared blood all over my driver's side door, and the police were looking at the blood. They then asked me about what had happened at the house with Daniel. I explained to them he had stabbed himself and was told I should not have left him alone. He could have died. I explained to them I was worried for my daughter's safety and my own. I had to leave; I was scared he was going to stab me or my daughter next. The police did not care about my side and proceeded to arrest me. They said how dare I leave him in a ditch bleeding alone. He could have died. So, after he stabbed himself in the neck, he then smeared blood all over my car, and then, to top it all off, he went and lay in the irrigation ditch along our street for someone to find him in such a manner.

Tawnie was driven to a friend's house by the police, and John was left to his own devices to find a way home all the way up the hill. I felt awful leaving them like that, but I had no choice. After I was booked and placed into jail, I contacted Daniel and told him he better make it right and tell the truth. Somehow, I got him to listen to my plea,, and he contacted the prosecutors, who released me and did not pick up charges against me. Being falsely charged started began to be an ongoing theme in my life I go on further into my story. You will begin to see the ridiculous number of times I have gone to jail. I have spent numerous times in jail for things I did not do. I am not saying I am perfect. I did a few things, and I take full responsibility. I did all the court papers and had all my records sealed and expunged before I started criminal justice. It is concerning to me because if they could do this to me this many times. My question was then, how many other innocent people had gone to prison because this cult had the power to make it happen? I even missed a great job opportunity through the Tuolumne County Department of Recreation. I had set an interview with. I missed this opportunity because Daniel stabbed himself.

In 2009, Daniel and I had been drinking at home, and we got into another fight after this incident. Instead of fighting with him, I decided to go out to his broke down B.M.W. in our driveway to listen to music. He had parked his truck behind the B.M.W., it, and I had parked my car beside it. There's no way the B.M.W. was going anywhere. Even though this car was broken down and didn't run, the radio still worked. I put the key in, enjoyed the music, and began having my own karaoke session. I was then accosted by the police tapping on the window with their flashlight. I rolled the window down and was asked to step out of the car. The officer asked if I had been drinking and was very honest with him, and I said, "yes." He then told me to turn around and arrested me for a D.U.I. I was blown away at the fact that I was not even attempting to drive but was still being arrested in my own driveway. Daniel must have called the police and told them I was drinking and, in the car, intentionally to cause me problems. I never would have thought in a million years that the person I loved was causing me harm. I know today how he was an intricate part of the set ups. My own husband, friends and family had been perpetuating on me for years. I took the D.U.I. ,completed the yearlong classes, and paid off the 10,000 dollars to keep my driver's license. I then had the D.U.I. on my driving record, which increased my car insurance for the next 10 years. A few years after this, I drove to Turlock one afternoon to visit my mother, Joanne Lair. She had cried to me about living in the streets. She had nowhere to live and asked me if she could come live with Daniel and me. Of course, I called Daniel right away and asked him if she could come live with us for a while. I was surprised that he said yes. I had her gather her things and took her back to Sonora with me. She stayed about 4 months, and then Daniel had said it was time for her to go. I sincerely felt for my mother, but I ended up dropping her back off in Turlock. I felt horrible when I had to drop her off at a park. As I drove away, I was crying.

Not only did Daniel lie to me about his nanny, but he also lied to me about his true legal name. In 2011, Four years into my marriage, we had been having multiple yard sales at some properties Daniel had inherited in Oakland, California, from his grandparents and an uncle who had committed suicide. These were neighboring homes side by side and took a long time to clean up. The homes he inherited were hoarder homes. His family was filthy and did not keep their homes up like normal people. We literally cleaned out these homes months and months before we could even start the remodel. Tons of garbage had to go. I also noticed piles of children's metal scooters. I mean a lot of them. It was very out of the ordinary. I now realize Daniel was sent into my life by this cult. Later in life, when the gang stalking began, I observed that this cult used tons of people on scooters they would use to create daily patterns. This was one of their tactics. I suppose when you see scooters everywhere you go, every day makes you wonder why so many of them were constantly around. It makes you start questioning your reality. I saw that this is exactly what they do. It's a way to get people confused and make you feel crazy. Plus, it is something so normal in the world, but if you go and tell someone scooters are always following you, you'd sound insane. I didn't realize how Daniel was connected until I started to think back when I began writing this book.

We had many yard sales. One weekend at the sale, a strange man from the neighborhood I had never seen approached Daniel. He began screaming at Daniel and addressing him, Alvin Diffie. Then, stating Daniel owed him money. Me being me, I tried to deescalate the situation and told this strange man that he was wrong and had the wrong person. He insisted Daniels's name was Alvin and attempted to physically fight him. I got between the two of them and broke up the situation. The man walked away, and they did not come to blows. That night, as we lay in bed, I began to ask Daniel why the strange man from the yard sale had called him Alvin. He then admitted to me that he was, in fact, not Daniel Melton and his true name was Alvin Diffie. He gave me a story about his dad being a Hells Angel who stole drugs from them, and they had killed his father, so his family moved him up to Tuolumne County. His aunt worked at the prison there and adopted him. She then changed his name to Daniel Melton. He lied to me about so much. I just kept forgiving him. I took my marriage seriously. All I know is I had changed my name to Shannon Melton, and I was sleeping with the enemy and didn't even know it. This had shattered all confidence in my marriage and a lot of things at this point. It made me question everything about this man I had decided to give my heart to. How could he lie about the nanny and then lied about his identity? Four years into my marriage, I had to find out from some random stranger at a yard sale the cold, hard truth. This was just another door in the halls of illusions that I had accidentally unlocked.

In 2011, I had told Daniel about my idea for a bra with pockets. He decided to fund my idea with the sale of the Oakland houses. I contacted a patient lawyer and then a patent company and got the ball rolling. I went through all the proper avenues to get the patent, and I made a prototype. Then, I sent it to the patient company. This process would take five years to accomplish. The completion of my patent was finalized in 2015. It's funny looking back because right after the certificate was completed and mailed to us. I framed it and put it on the wall and then was arrested and sent to prison and sentenced to nine years and eight months. Unbeknownst to Daniel, I had already started the divorce process before the arrest. I was leaving him, and he wasn't having it. While in jail waiting to go to prison, I received the finalization of my divorce and what a blessing that was.

CHAPTER 2

WAKING UP

I was in the county jail in Tuolumne County jail, facing nine years and eight months, being charged with assault with a deadly weapon and corporal injury on a spouse. I was finally fed up and had moved out of most of my things. When he realized I was finally leaving, he came at me and attacked me. I had to hit him with my hair dryer. I had only hit him one time. For my protection and to get him out of my way, I had to help myself. The seven years of abuse I had endured during my marriage was pure hell. I would always call the police when Daniel would beat me and start tearing our house apart. They would come, but he would never get arrested. Once, the Sonora Police Department was contacted by the hospital staff. I was found hiding behind the Elks Lodge across from our house. When one of the members found me, I was bleeding from the top of my head with blood all over my face and hair. He called 911, and an ambulance came to take me to the hospital to get staples in a 14-inch gash on the top of my head. The police only took a report, but there was no arrest. After all the disregard from law enforcement for my safety, I felt I had to protect my own life. I had moved out most of my things when Daniel had left for arraigns. I was putting on my makeup in the bathroom when he arrived home, and he immediately noticed my things were gone. I also had boxes ready to pack the rest of my things. He went crazy. Started calling me a whore and just speaking to me with pure disdain I could tell he was raging. When he got to a certain point in his mania, there was no coming back. I saw the blank, empty, demonic glare come across his eyes. This was a look I had frequently seen when he would hurt me. I grabbed my hair dryer and twirled the cord around as if I were Zena the Princess Warrior. The plug in part of the hair dryer hit his forehead, and he grabbed his head and was crying. This was my opportunity to save myself. I ran out of the front door and quickly got into my car. I backed up like a speed racer and left. It was one good whack, and he didn't even go to the hospital. He had one little nik on his forehead. He had beaten me so many times before, and I was in fear for my life and had no other option but to save myself. The hands of a psychopath were hands that had been laid upon me too many times, and this would be the last time.

Weeks before, I met a man named Darren. I had shared with him the trauma I was enduring from my husband. After hearing my horror stories, he felt bad for me, and he invited me to come stay with him. Darren's house was where I had moved my stuff to the day prior to my arrest. He was a prospect from the Hells Angels, and I felt I would be safe with him and his group of friends he hung around. I only had gotten the impression that The Hells Angels were protectors. My mother Joanne used to leave me for weeks at a time with strangers in their cult when I was a baby in diapers. She would not come back for weeks at a time. I was too small to remember those incidents, but I was definitely abused. As I grew older, my mother tried to make me think these kinds of people were ok to trust. Darren had lived in the back area of his brother's closed snowboard shop that was full of their products but just unproductive. It was closed. It was an office building with only office rooms and a small office bathroom with a toilet and sink. No shower or tub. One office room was his bedroom, with just a mattress on the floor and a few of his clothes. One other office room was a kitchen with a hot plate, a refrigerator and a small table. He had a few shelves to put food on and stuff, but it was a rough issue. All the dishes had to be taken to the backyard to be washed in the hoes he had set up as a wash station. This station was also for showers. I would spray him, and he would spray me with the water hose. The point I am trying to get across is. I knew I was leaving my comfortable home, materially, with my fake husband. I knew I needed to be uncomfortable for change to occur in my life. I was done being abused. I did not care that it was going to be a little harder on basics and survival. I knew if I were to stay, he was going to kill me. After I hit Daniel, I drove to Darren's house and stayed the night with him. The next morning, when I went back to Daniels, I was arrested. Right when I arrived to pack up the last of my things. The police showed up, and I was arrested. I called Darren from the jail, and he called Alladin Bail Bonds and came to bail me out. I had thought

Darren was a nice guy, but after a few months of living with him, his true colors eventually came out. He ended up physically abusing me as well. I seemed to keep getting put in the cycle of violence with any relationship I was in. I did not even know about the cycle of violence trauma I was in; I just thought that was normal life. Men hit you, and then they care. Such horrible programming. A few months went by, and I was stressing the fact that I was facing so many charges and such a long sentence. I didn't deserve it. My public defender did not want to go to trial. I wanted to. He stresses, and the anxiety were creeping in on me. One night, he started to fight with me ,slammed me up against the wall and choked me. He grabbed me by the throat, lifted me off the ground, and slammed me up against the wall. This freaked me out that he was now abusing me as well. I reacted and hit him back in defense. His house was in the back of a snow board shop, and the door was very heavy, like a grocery store door. He pushed me down on the ground opened the door and let it go right onto my forehead, causing it to split wide open. The metal door then split my forehead open and peeled the skin off from my eyebrow to my hairline. There was blood everywhere and all over my face. I had bleached blonde hair at this time, and my hair was red from the amount of blood on it. In fear, I called 911 on my cell phone. The ambulance and police came. The funny thing about this story is I was the one who left in an ambulance, but I was arrested. The police never arrested him for what he had done to me. Being out on bail already, I was then charged with a bail enhancement and had my bail raised so high I couldn't bail out again, left to face all my charges behind bars. At my next court hearing, my public defender told me I was facing 11 years off the top.

While I was in jail and waiting to attend my due process, I had met a woman who was having good luck in court for some pretty harsh charges and was waiting to be picked up by another state for similar charges. She would talk about God and, every night, would encourage us to gather in order to read something called a daily devotional. I had no clue what it was or about. I simply just saw that things were going well for her and decided I wanted to try this God thing out… This woman was not your typical bible thumper or preachy type, but God uses anybody he can, and he sure used her to bring me into the kingdom. What she was sharing with me was something I had never heard of or even thought about. One night, after we had read the devotional, all the other women crawled into their beds and cuddled in for the night. I was left in the middle of the room, sitting on a cold metal steel table, feeling lost and alone. I had come to the lowest I had ever been before. I began to cry as as I sat in the solitude of my tears. The Lord came to me and physically touched my chin. I literally felt as if a giant index finger had been placed upon my face, and he lifted my head to the heavens. When this was transpiring, I simply couldn't fathom what was taking place in my life. I looked around the room in utter amazement. I couldn't believe that was happening to me. I looked around the room to see if anyone else was seeing what was happening. God had come to me, and he showed up and showed out. None of the other women were aware of what had happened. Without any words, I was understanding exactly what was being said to me. He said," Daughter don't cry. I love you; I am here for you! Please do not hang your head in sorrow, but look up to me. I am waiting for you. The Lord's finger had been placed upon my chin and lifted my head towards the heavenly realms as if he was saying don't cry, and I am here for you. I have never looked back since. His promises of hope and a future filled with love were unheard of until this point in my life. I was in. The first book I read was The Battlefield of the Mind" By Joyce Meyers. This book also had a workbook that came with it, and it opened my spiritual eyes for the first time. I was so enthralled with the knowledge I was gaining about the devil and how he attacks our minds first. The devil was something I never really had thought about before reading this book. I am so glad some one had given me this book to read because it began the renewing of my mind.

This was a defining moment for me. I knew I wanted more, something bigger, and I was never looking back. While in prison, I spent every opportunity to grow in His word, and I would attend all religions and spirituality services offered. I wanted to see which one was the right fit for me. I felt the truth in the word of Christ and that Jesus died for my sins on the cross and then resurrected on the third day. Even though I had no guidance in His word previously, I knew I was going to stand up for my newfound Father. I knew deep down inside God would show me what was right and guide me, and boy, did He ever! I constantly listened to Christian music and completely stopped listening to mainstream music. The people that were coming to share the word were very kind and reliable. I looked forward to all of them coming. They did not have to do this, but they chose to come and spread the word of Christ with the so-called undesirables of society. My soul was being fed by every psalm, every proverb and every story of the bible. We would even have discussions on longsuffering. There were a lot of discussions on the topic. Longsuffering sounded horrible, but when you come to understand, lean not on your own understanding, and everything happens for a reason. You can begin to understand that God has a plan, and His plan is better than ours. Longsuffering is how we grow into the people He needs us to be. Many are called, and few are chosen. I still went full in with God, knowing that we must go through pain to find our purpose. Maybe that's why most people decide to turn from the call and go through the wide gates and not the narrow ones. It's easy to not follow God's commandments. It's easy to follow the devil. You must ask yourself why, and there's probably a reason for this. Most people don't think they just do impulsively. I knew his promises were true, and I had found the truth. Seek, and you shall find; knock, and He will open the door. I had never experienced such unconditional love, and the devil had lied to me and stole all my happiness. I was done with the devil. I just was not aware of the chains he had placed on every aspect of my life. As I learned the way of the Lord, I grew to be more patient, kind, and understanding and gained the fruits of the spirit. I felt him taking away all the anger, loneliness, abandonment and sadness I held inside of me. He took away all the trauma I had gone through during my childhood. He was healing me from the inside out. There was a class every Saturday I would attend. It was my favorite class. It was five hours long, and it was all about the word of Christ and Jesus, basically theology. We had conversations about the bible and its stories and how to integrate the use of this knowledge into our daily lives. The instructor asked us what the one bible verse we used daily, and he split us up into groups. We had to make a poster and a presentation, which he turned into a contest. The winners got to take a group photo and be placed in a prison community magazine. My group decided to use the verse" The Armor of God." This is a weapon He has given to all of us as warriors and soldiers of Christ. If I use the tools we are given, we are more than prepared to fight back in the spiritual realm. I learned by girding myself with this entire supernatural Armor of God that no weapon formed against me shall prosper. My group ended up winning, and I got to take my first prison pose picture with all the lifers in my group. I was the only non-lifer who attended this class, but I truly enjoyed the other women in the class and did not judge anyone. We were all there, and all were striving for change.

The situations at church were not always ideal. There would always be drug dealers or women homosecting in the bathrooms. They would even come to sit in the congregation area, trying to talk loudly and be disrespectful. I am the kind of person who hates disrespectful people, especially in the house of God. I would stand up for the people who came for the church and had taken time out of their busy lives for us to to share the word. These inmates were usually lifers who had no respect or consideration for anyone. Most of these women didn't really like when I would expose their rude and inexcusable behavior. I had no problem sticking up for the other women who were there to learn. I always put them on blast in front of the room. I would think, "Oh, not in MY GODS HOUSE". That's when God showed me his power and how he is our vengeance. Those women the next week would be publicly excused from the services, and I knew God was the one behind the embarrassment. I eventually stopped worrying about others in the church not acting right because God would take care of it every time after that. I used to sit and smile when he would show me how He had my back.

While attending church services, I met so many women in pain like I had been. When I looked into their eyes, I saw myself looking back. I knew even though I was new in the world. I needed to bring encouragement and joy into their hearts. As I drew closer to God, it seemed like more and more women would come to me for prayers and to vent their pains and concerns. I felt honored comfortable how comfortable they felt coming to me. My heart cried for these women. It brought me joy to remind these women how smart, bright and beautiful they truly were. I knew how it felt myself deep down but just didn't realize how neglected I had been as a child. Looking back now, I had never been told I was loved or supported by anyone in my family. I had just ignored the fact that my family couldn't or wouldn't give me words of love and encouragement. I always had to be my own cheerleader. These encounters only let me see that I was not alone in the neglect that I had experienced and endured. I participated in the first water baptism that had ever been offered at The California Institution for Women. I was so excited the day it came. I knew I was turning my life around and giving my soul to Christ. I felt like I was marrying the Lord. I knew this would mean I would be stepping into His full grace, and I was going to become a child of The Most High forever, not by force, but willing, by my own choice. My free will. He was welcoming me into His family, a family that I had been hidden away from me. My turn came to step into the renewing waters of Christ. I stepped in feet first and slowly sat down in the cold Holy water. Even though the water was cold, I was engulfed in the warmth of the Lord. When the pastor laid me back, I began to pray. I was releasing the person I was before I knew Him. I was becoming a new person in Christ. I gave myself to Him without any question or hesitation. Everything about my experience felt right.

I was enveloped in His powerful, loving force. I felt His presence with me in the water at that moment. Utter peace and bliss rushed through my entire body. For the first time in my life, I felt peace, love, kindness, caring, consideration, and understanding all at once. I had pledged my soul to the Most High. When I brought myself up out of the healing waters and stepped out of the bath. The next woman in line, whom I had never met before, told me," Oh my gosh, it was so beautiful when you were under the water you had a glow and a glittery sparkle around you. Also, the birds started singing louder." I thought she was just being nice, but I took her compliment and said thank you for the observation. I had been training myself in hopes of entering the Cal Fire Program. This is a program offered to inmates who want to help the community instead of sitting around in the prison system. Stuck with lifers like Leslie Vanhousen, one of the Manson sisters, basically a bunch of violent and ruthless killers. In this program, you can make a difference in the community and yourself, as well as make a dollar an hour on each fire you work on. While on fires, you get fire meals, including steaks, chicken, burgers and fries. Real food! You get treated like a real person, with respect by the officers and the public. People often sights ask for pictures of our crews out on hikes or at work sites. We also participated in community projects at a camp for blind children. Trimming the trees and cutting overgrown foliage ensured no injuries for the children when they rode the horses. This is a program offered to certain criteria of inmates. I was 320 pounds from the pill concoction the marriage counselor prescribed for me. I learned from the medical staff in jail that the medications I was taking were deadly when mixed together. It should have killed me. Plus, I was drinking tons of alcohol on top of them. Miracle, I am here still, they told me. Thank God I did not die from it though. Guess my family was involved in that little fiasco as well.

When I arrived at the California Institute for Women and began to run daily and practice the required exercises needed to pass the physical fitness portion of the testing, I had to run a mile in 9 minutes 30 sec mile, do 5 minutes of stepping boxes on each leg, 25 sit-ups and 20 burpees. We also had to do a 3-mile pack out with a 50-pound pack on to ensure we were strong enough for the fire gear. Not to mention the crazy hikes we had to endure with treacherous names like the Stair Way to Heaven or the Devil's Backbone which is kind of ironic if you think about it.

I ended up losing 120 pounds and became very fit. I pushed myself and experienced a moment in my life that not many people can accomplish. It is very hard to get into camp, and not many people pass. I give God all the glory for my perseverance in this situation. When I was doing my pack out, I saw some hawks flying around and noticed one on top of the light post. As I came around the last lap of my pack out, I felt God celebrating my accomplishment. He left me a gorgeous feather that had fallen off one of the hawks. I knew this was a gift from God just for me. Even though I was being timed, I quickly bent down and snatched it up with a smile on my face, and it brought joy to my heart. It gave me the motivation to go harder and finish strong. It was yet another magical moment that God made me feel special. He was cheering me on and saying keep going, daughter, you've got this. God had put me through pain and strife, but it was all worth it. This accomplishment showed me I had more in me that I was not aware of until I pulled it out of the debts of my soul. It had changed something inside me, and I began to trust in Him more and more. I kept that feather for many years until my son threw it away when the MKULTRA harassment began. I am not going to lie about . It destroyed me when it was gone. This gift was from the love of God. How could they steal something that was priceless? They don't understand a feather it is priceless. they are so materialistic; only diamond rings, Ferraris, and Rock Revival jeans are priceless gifts! They sell their souls for a pair of Rock Revival jeans! They could never understand the true gifts in life.

I decided to challenge the course, which meant that I didn't have to go through 6 weeks in PFT, physical fitness training, with the lifers who were given jobs as physical fitness trainers. These women were sentenced to life in prison, and this was their paid job, so they were obviously physically fit and had no mercy on us. I challenged the course and passed it with flying colors. I did it to perfection in my eyes, and the next week, I found myself in Malibu, Ca. on the beach. WHHATTT!!! Can you imagine being sent to prison? Which is horrific off the top! But then God sends you to Malibu, California, on the beach. Not only was I on a fire crew, but I was also appointed the L.A. County Fire Department's Fire Captains clerk. This position involved completing required paperwork for paying the inmates, incoming emergency calls, sending the crews on calls, maintaining equipment, and handing out the equipment to the crews as needed. This job also helped me grow in my leadership skills, which I never knew I had. It was as if I fell into my element. I really appreciated the fact that I was not in a real prison. I was helping the community and learning things about myself at the same time. We were forced to participate in daily timed hikes, sometimes holding our tools and equipment. If I hadhad not completed the hike in the required time, the consequence would have been a 115, which meant more time was added to your sentence. So, I stayed on point when it came to hiking. I hurt my ankle one day, which had been injured years prior. I was sent back to prison and had my medical status changed to non-grade. Being non-grade meant that you were no longer on the crew and would be working only on the campgrounds without having to maintain the physical aspects of being at camp. I was reassigned to Puerta La Cruz in San Diego, California. This camp gave me the lead of clothing and laundry. This job only requires one person, which was nice because I didn't have to deal with other coworkers and having any issues. At the same time, the crews would be gone out on fire calls, which would sometimes last for months. I would be the only one left at camp in the crew area. The kitchen crew had their own quarters along with the kitchen crew. Totaling around 8 women at the camp. This was a time of relaxation and rest. This time also gave me more time to go within and be with God. My role in this position was also to greet the new inmates who were coming into the camp every Friday. I always tried to make the new women feel comfortable being in the new environment. I would give them a tour of the camp and how things were ran. I quite enjoyed Fridays, and meeting the newbies, gave me great pleasure.

While at Puerta La Cruz, I continued to go to church. The church that came to this camp was just amazing. They were not like any of the other churches that I had been attending. Most of the other churches would come to share only the basic knowledge of the Word, but these individuals were pure spiritual warriors. Filled with the Holy spirit, unlike anything I have ever seen. We were in their church, and this aspect made me feel very grateful. I felt as if they took me under their wings. They were a couple named Kim and Tom, and occasionally they would bring an older couple to share the word and healing with us named Dick and Jane.

Dick had stated he had healing hands, and he would come he would lay hands on us. They also shared how to speak in tongues and not feel restricted by any judgment when doing so. Dick put his hands on my shoulders one Sunday and said he could see I was a healer. I also had healing hands. When he placed his hands upon me, he began to whisper in my ear what he has seen. He said that, "I see you sitting around a big table at a meeting with important people." I thought he was kind, and I didn't understand what he was talking about at the time. I took in his information and gracefully appreciated what he had shared with me. I always kept what he said in my mind even though it seemed so not like something I would be a part of. On Wednesday nights, another couple would come and talk about how they would have people that were demon possessed would come into their home, and they would perform exorcisms on them. They would teach us about generational curses and evil spirits like depression, suicide, succubus, incubus, sexual immorality, root curses and how to break generational curses. They also spoke of how demons can attach themselves to us and our lives. I was given lesson packets to do during the week, and I always took the time to complete them. I gained so much knowledge and awareness. I was shocked to learn that such things were real in this world. I took the information in hopes I would never have to use it.

They would talk about how giant angels would enter their homes. These angels were so big and tall their heads would tower through the roof of their home. Glowing and shining so brightly. They would interact with them so lovingly and peacefully but were there to help in the process they were accomplishing. I am not going to lie. At the time I really thought these people were a little crazy, but I listened to what they had to say and took the knowledge in. I filed it in the back of my mind just in case I needed it in the future. Never thought I would have to sort through these files ,pull them out and use them for myself.

At least I was aware of spiritual warfare but never expected it to happen to me. It's like watching these horrible news stories that only happen to other people. I thought it couldn't or wouldn't happen to me. Especially when I was released from prison and how it did come upon me in the manner it did. It came upon me with full force. I know God had been me training me for what was to come while I was in prison. Every aspect had been preparing me for the demonic assault the was coming for me in the future. Being in prison is an all-around extremely loud environment. I simply would use ear plugs to block out the noise and learned to simply ignore it all. Most of the time I slept with my headphones on with Gospel music blasting all night. I was taking good vibes and listening to songs in my sleep. I woke up yelling Diamonds out of Dust, which is a song. Another night, I yelled Revival and sat straight up in my bed. Then, being in a fire camp, I was around loud chainsaws and weed whackers all day, which are very noisy on top of everything else in the environment. When the gang stalking began, they would attack me with noise harassment. So, when I would start to feel my peace being disturbed, I would pop in a set of earplugs. Even if I had to use bread, which works very well, by the way! I can declare I was completely prepared for spiritual warfare. The Freemasons would have won and gotten exactly what they wanted, which was my soul, but God had other plans. They did not put God in their equation when they plotted against my life.

Puerta la Cruz was in Warner Springs, California, which meant that we had no opportunity for self-help classes. The camp was located so far out of the city limits that not many people would even venture out that far. I was really interested in taking self- help classes because I knew I had nothing in common with most of the women in my circumstance. I was not a criminal in any way, shape or form, and I wanted to learn all about why I ended up in prison. I also wanted to make sure I didn't end up incarcerated again. I had a meeting with committee. This is a board of people that can decide the locations of your incarceration. I requested to be transferred to Folsom prison in Sacramento, California. This prison was a short-term prison, which meant all the women had out dates. I would also be closer to my family and really wanted to see my grandchildren. I had not seen them in over 2 ½ years. I was 9 months to the gate and really felt it was the best thing to do. I knew it was a rougher environment and less advantageous. Even though it would be harder on me. I had to do it to learn more about myself. The camp was a luxury, and everyone thought I was crazy for leaving. I am just the kind of person who would rather endure a rough situation to gain myself and gain self-knowledge than be comfortable. Plus, I could go home a few months earlier by taking these courses. It was like killing two birds with one stone. By taking self-help classes, I could earn a milestone, which meant I would get time off my sentence. I didn't take the class. I truly wanted to learn about myself. I took all faith-based classes and a drug dependency class for that reason that was 6 months long. It was called S.A.P. Substance Abuse Program, and this was a class in a group setting. Most inmates were required to take this class, but it was not a requirement for me. I wanted to participate on my own. I was then asked to be a big sister in the program as well, which was an honor for me. My job as a big sister was to greet the new women coming into the program. I would take them down the hallway to meet all the counselors available to us. I would explain how the program went and the schedule during our days. I was excited to be invited to be a big sister, and I would try to help motivate the women who did not really want to be in the program. I wanted them to feel comfortable and tried to make it seem not so bad.

Every evening, I took faith-based classes and was also an aid in these classes. I took Beyond Trauma, Parenting, Boundaries, 5 love Languages, Codependency, and Sacred Secrets. These classes gave me so much enlightenment and knowledge as to things I had no idea about myself and really helped me heal. After taking Boundaries, I had an epiphany and began to use my boundaries, and I must say this was the most important class I took out of them all. This was something I never knew I could do. I realized that having boundaries does not mean it's a way to self-preserve. If I can tell any of you anything. I want to say boundaries are the true way to master yourself. Before taking this class, I let people walk all over me. I had always put myself aside before this class. I learned that I could say no and that it was not a bad thing. It is ok to be selfish with yourself. Other people should not come before your own beliefs and happiness. How can you be any good to the world if you're depleted and drained by the wants and needs of others.

The crazy part of me landing in Folsom Prison was that I had been at work at Taco Bell. And I got a text message from my mom saying that my sister was in the hospital

Not just in the hospital but in intensive care. She had been stabbed 14 times. With her long punctured and her head almost severed. I immediately left work and went to her rescue. I was horrified by what I saw when I arrived and stood by her side for a few days. She finally came out of the coma they had induced upon her. And started to recover Her and our mother and her. I had thought for sure My sister had lived a pretty rough life on the streets. And I thought this was going to be the turning point. Now she's gonna change her life. It was crazy because the first moment my mother showed up ,my sister began to talk to her. They started to discuss how my sister wanted to smoke a cigarette. I had told them both if they went outside to smoke a cigarette with Cassie's lung punctured like that, I was not going to have anything to do with them from this point on. And that was exactly what I did because they proceeded to put Cassie into a wheelchair and went outside and smoked cigarettes. I did leave. For the moment. But when Cassie needed a ride out of the hospital, I was the one who came and picked her up. Unbeknownst to me. She had told me to drop her off at the same place where she had been stabbed. I cannot believe that she requested to go back to the same place that almost had destroyed her. As I dropped her off, I noted in my mind the smoking of the cigarette, the disregard for her own life, going back to the same place that she almost died at, and I swore to myself I was not going to be around this toxic family. I haven't spoken to my sister for about a year. As time went by in my horrible marriage. And I caught my case. As I was sitting in the county jail. I was thinking back to the point of my sister's assault. I knew the woman had been sentenced to seven years in prison. And I figured at some point in time, I might run across this woman. The funny thing is. When I got to Folsom, there she was. She lived the tier below me. And I would hear her name called on the loudspeaker daily. But,being the older sister to Cassie, no one really knew that I was alive. I was 10 years older than Cassie, and this woman had no clue that Cassie even had an older sister. As she would walk by me, I would think I could get her and I could attack her, I could hurt her for what she did to my sister. But you know, I had God in my heart, and God said just forgive her. I had to do that constantly, every day. Just forgive her, Just forgive her. Just forgive her. One evening, we were sitting watching television in the group room, and she leaned over to me and asked me where I was from. I replied. Ohh, I'm from Turlock. She said. Ohh, Turlock, I might know your family. And I said, ohh, you know my family. And began to say Cassie's lair. She immediately grabbed my hand and started crying. She pulled me to a table so we could speak alone. She admitted her wrongs to me, and she had pleaded with me about her guilt. And begged me to forgive her. And I exclaimed, I do forgive you, and so does God. She and I actually became closer, and I moved down to the tier where she lived. She was two weeks to the gate. And when she left, she left me all the things that she had in her locker and that I could use. I had vowed to myself I was not going to ever tell my sister about the relationship that I had found in prison with the woman who almost murdered her. Because deep down inside, I knew my sister didn't know God, and she would not understand the forgiveness that I had in my heart for what had occurred.

I must say but not bragging, I felt I was the epidemy of rehabilitation. Other women in prison would make fun of me and call me Polley the Programmer. Finally, for the first time in my life, I had no hate, anger or frustration. I finally felt in control of myself and my actions for the first time ever. I felt equipped for the future, and God had a huge place in my heart. What the devil meant for bad, God took and made it for my good. Just as he promised me. I was released in 2018 and went to stay with my paternal grand-mother, Marylin Hayes and her husband, Frank Martin. Frank never liked me the entire 20 something years he was married to my grandmother. He never seemed to give up the past and was always bringing it up. I had to block out the negativity that was being projected onto me right from the gate when I got home. He never seemed to want to give me a chance. My grandmother welcomed me into her home, and she had a room decorated with many beautiful things. And made me feel comfortable and right at home. I felt so happy to finally be with my family. I loved them very much. The first night I was home, my son Austin came to pick me up. We went to eat at Apple Bees and then to a movie.

He took me to see Spiderman, the animated version of 2018. I now know that his picking this movie was ironic because later down the road, my father would ask me if I saw Spiderman walking through our neighborhood. I had not seen anyone in our neighborhood dressed like Spider-man, and if I have, I sure would have went to my kids and told them about it. When the gang stalking began, I noticed Spiderman was another pattern these people used to get me to go crazy. This is just another aspect of the patronization of weirdness they use. Not aware of what was to come in the future. I just thought, cool, Spiderman…

I had not seen my boy in so long, and so when he walked up the stairs and his face peered over the staircase, I began to cry. My little boy was no longer a teenager but a full-grown man. I wiped the tears from my eyes and gave him a big hug. He was a grown man with a big red beard. I greeted him with loving arms. I was back with my boy and felt whole again. We shared a wonderful evening together, and he really made me believe that he had true love for me. I had raised him alone and thought we had a great relationship, even though we had a major hiccup when he was 14. I was his mom and his dad, even though I was not the best disciplinary parent. I would always let him off being grounded early. I also had learned what a sexist parent is. I made my girls do the dishes, but not Austin. I only required him to take out the garbage. Even when he did not do that, I would end up taking it out for him. All he did was play video games, which were not cheap. I would spend hundreds of dollars on these games only for him to finish them in three days. I had no clue what was to come in the next few years from my own son, whom I loved and adored with all my heart.

CHAPTER 3
LIVING MY LIFE, DISCOVERING HORROR

Things were going well for me. I had my patent on my mind. I had some intentions of following through with my project. Being that I had been thrown into prison right when I could have gone to the next level with it. I did not have the resources or funds to go on into manufacturing. I contacted the patent office and getting the information in the hopes of the future. My ex-husband had kept the official original documents and paperwork and, so I would have to start all over to receive a copy of it. Plus, my grandmother was always saying," I think someone already made that product," and she was always shooting down my dreams. I couldn't understand why she would never support me. She never believed in my dreams; she would only tear them down. She was not one to cheer me on in my endeavors. My future happiness was just something she used to hurt me with harsh words of discouragement.

While I was married to get on Facebook or any kind of website on the computer. When I came home from prison,

I decided to make a new Facebook, and I started receiving messages from different individuals. One particular message I received was from a really hot Military guy who used to send me hot pictures of himself. I did have a gay friend at the time who had moved to Maine, and we just talked sporadically. One day, we were talking, and he was in a bad mood,, so I told him to let me send you something that'll make you feel better. So, I sent him the picture of this military guy. My friend Brian then alerted me to the fact that I had been catfished?. I stated that I had catfished. What is that? I had no clue what catfishing was. I really thought this person was real and wanted to talk to me. I then quickly realized that he was right because the person never ever called me on the phone, and I could never call him. This began a year long journey with a person who was completely fraudulent and portrayed to be 10 different people that I thought were reputable citizens in the world. First, he was a bridge builder. Then he was a doctor. He was the military guy. He was a guy in the military who just couldn't talk to me. He was many different aspects of different people. In the end, he ended up using Vin Diesel, the actor. I had to go get my daughter Hannah. Because I wanted her to see that Vin Diesel was calling me and talking to me on Facebook. My daughter always assumed I was gullible and used to tell me that I shouldn't believe everything that I see on TV, like the commercials for products that you see on late night television. So, I went to her in hopes that I could get some validation. She came and saw my messages, and he had even her believing that he was Vin Diesel in the end. He wasn't lol. A couple of weeks after this, I received a phone call from somebody from

Haiti, Africa. He had told me he was the person behind all the fraudulent accounts and pretended people for the entire year. He then told me he felt awful and bad because he saw I was a good person and I didn't deserve to be treated in such a manner. He then begged for my forgiveness. He asked me to please forgive him and could I please be his friend. He then proceeded to send me pictures of himself. And asking me if we can be friends on my level as a real person. I definitely wasn't interested in being someone's friend who had just deceived me for an entire year. I thought he was crazy, and I thought he needed help. I simply explained to him no, I don't want to be your friend. ,timeI hung up the phone, and that was the last time I had ever heard from this person. Crazy stuff, right? Who pretends to be somebody they're not? I had no clue. That this was going on in the world, was just the beginning of the first parade of lies and sinister jokes that were being put into my life. Without me even understanding the true reality of what they were doing.

Life goes on. So, I put an ad on indeed.com, and I found a job for a Christian camp that was hiring a kitchen crew. I was hired on the day of my interview. I was completely honest with my boss about my prison stay and how I found God while there. He respected my honesty and understood the fact that I was abused by my husband. His niece had almost been killed by her abusive husband and could relate to my situation. He would all gather every morning and read the bible and discuss the daily word. And we also ate lunch together every afternoon as well. They became my second family. I loved my coworkers. I had moved up to lead of the kitchen in a few months and was given awesome benefits as well. I had medical, dental and paid sick days. It was the best job that I had ever landed in my entire life... I would cook for 300 to 400 children or adults and loved it. The camp counselors would often pull me out of the kitchen, and the children would say," Thank you, Ms. Shannon". Then, she would have them asked me questions. It was a fun time. The property was private land, and strangers were not supposed to be on the property with or without guests there. No one authorized was to be on the property. But I started to notice odd people wandering around the property and couldn't understand why these people would randomly be walking around. I didn't ever say anything to the individuals, but I did bring it to my bosses' attention. He told me no one was to be on the property at any times and I should speak up to these people when I saw them, but I never did. Now that I have become awakened to my family's occult connections, I see that it was just their members coming to check in on my life. One day, around this time, I received a letter in the mail from the California Department of Corrections and Rehabilitation. The letter had stated that someone not authorized had fraudulently broken into my medical records. It was an apology letter from the state for their mistake. I did not think anything of it until after all this other stuff started occurring a few years down the road.

My uncle Byron had been living at my father's home up in Twain Harte Ca with my two grown children. Austin and Hannah. I was still living at my grandma Marylin's home and doing quite well. My son and my uncle began to have arguments and physical fights. On the first Christmas

I was back home, I was happy to have my entire family come together. But when it came time for our celebration, Byron hit my son, and they did not even show up at the party. Yet another disappointment. Uncle Byron eventually moved out, which meant there was room at my father's house open. After this fight, my son began to ask me to move from my grandmother's home and move over to my father's house with him and Hannah. Austin had a girlfriend that lived with him supposedly unknown to my father. It was a room that my father used to grow his marijuana in. This room was like a basement room with cement walls and was not really a part of the main home. I didn't really like his girl. Every time I had gone over to visit, she would be naked on the bed with a blanket covering her. Mind you, my son was very handsome and attractive and could have any woman that he wanted, but somehow, he had chosen this overweight, lazy, fat witch. She had stated she was a witch herself, which was the main reason for my dislike of her. She was a bad influence on my son's wellbeing. One day, my son and I had a discussion. He had told me he was worried about the whole world imploding in on itself and then almost having a panic attack. I thought this was such an odd thing to worry about when there are real problems in the world. His girlfriend was also very dirty and never cleaned anything, and would leave her menstrual blood all over the toilet. And if I would mention anything to her about these situations, it would be a huge fight with my son. So, I was hesitant to move over to my father's house. But eventually, I did. Things were going well between myself and my children. Good times like singing together as we had done when they were kids.

Watching movies and saying movie quotes was a thing we did a lot. We were silly. My oldest daughter even let me watch my two granddaughters a lot after work. This was a big part of my life. I loved spending time with them. My job required me to be there at 5 a.m., so I would go to bed around 7 a.m. every night. I began to hear sexual noises in the house around 12 a.m. nightly but thought it was me just dreaming or something. But it was happening so much that I began to record these incidents with my phone. I then listened to these recordings over and over just to make sure I was really hearing what I was hearing. I recognized my children's voices, along with my father. I could hear the bed and the floor screeking with the sexual acts being done in the house. This house was a cabin-style house, which made every noise and bump very easy to hear. I was destroyed when I realized what I was hearing with my own two ears. I had not wanted to work when they were little because the thought of leaving them with strangers who would molest them just killed me. I never left my kids with strangers, only my family members. I did not leave them often either. Very rare. It all makes sense now because when my kids were small, my entire family was constantly talking down on me to my children, and I couldn't understand why because I was a wonderful and loving parent to all 3 of my children. Once, even when they were small, his wife called one of the people I was dating and was talking crap about me to him. I did end up hitting her. And I did go to jail. It was either the choice of sending my kids to CPS or letting my family take them, and I chose my family because they're my family, and I never thought they would hurt my children. My kids were kept from me without supervised visits for about a year, and then I got my children back after working very hard and jumping through hoops to accomplish this. In 2004, I even went back to high school and graduated with a diploma. Not a G.E.D. I needed to do it the right way. I even got a cap and gown and walked in the ceremony. It was a big day for me. I had to strive in life, and I had created out of my own motivation to make things better. I had no support or motivation from anyone on either side of my family. I wanted to show my children that even if you can't do things at a certain time in your life, you can do them later. I was a teen mother and needed to show my children. The things no one had ever shown me. The right thing to do, even an attempt to be successful. I yerned for basic guidance but had to learn on my own.

So, for me to hear my children on the recordings being raped and harmed by the same person who had always tried so hard to keep a wall between us, pieces of the puzzles from the past were now beginning to make a little more sense. I was utterly disgusted, and broken at the same time. Because I had entrusted my children to my own family, and they did everything they could to betray that trust. I was totally disgusted by the fact that the ones closest to me ended up using my children for their sick and evil pleasures. At the time, I didn't understand the extent of this true evil that had incased my life. I kept what I had stumbled upon to myself. Questioning all the events that possibly could occur if I were to expose this abuse. The secrets that were never to be known were now known by me. I could not swallow the disgusting acts that were being done to my children. I knew if I made this known to any one family or friend, no one would believe me. I did have the recordings. I needed to do something, but I was not quite sure how to proceed at the moment. A little back-story is.

Around 2014, while married to Daniel. My son was 14, and he had been in his room for 3 days, and I grew concerned. So, when he went into the bathroom, I went and snuck into his room. I grabbed his laptop, and what was on his screen horrified me. What he had been looking at was a comic/cartoon version of sadomasochistic acts being done to a woman. Vaginas being cut with razor blades, breasts with bob wire wrapped them tightly, bloody scenes that I couldn't fathom. I flipped out and almost caught my first felony due to the argument that ensued when I showed my son what I saw he was up to. I was arrested and faced with time. At the time, I couldn't understand why he would be looking at such things and knew someone had to of shown him this stuff. Kids aren't born interested in these acts. I really looked towards his abuser as possibly his bus driver from school. The man named Sunny was always being a little too nice to my boy. That was a little too over friendly with my boy. Never in a million years did I ever even have the thought it was my own blood doing it to my children. EVER.... Things were not the same between us for long long time. He began to run away from home and be very rebellious towards me, too. Due to the past situations with him as well, I really didn't know how I was going to approach my father with it. I felt as if I would not have any backup for my discovery from other family members. I knew I would face persecution if I were to mention these acts.

I already knew my father was strange. As a child, I was snooping through his room and found a lost stuffed animal of mine under his waterbed mattress. When I found it, I was glad to have come across it, at first, but as I looked at it. It had the arm cut off with a roll-on deodorant stuck in the arm with a pair of my underwear around it. I was naturally confused as to what this was that I had found. I have never spoken about this to anyone until now writing about it in this book. He also had shared with me that he killed his boy scout leader with his friends when they got older. He said they threw his body into the aqueduct. I was scared by the information he told me and immediately went to my best friend Melisa, who was also my step cousin on my mother's side, to vent to her about what he had told me. Over the years, Melisa and I would often discuss his crime and try to figure out if it was, in fact, true. Also, my dad took Melisa and me to an ACDC concert when I was 12 years old. I had no clue who ACDC was. Melissa had just gotten her driver's permit, and I was glad that she had got to drive the car to the concert. When we were at the concert, my father brought his binoculars. I thought he looked very awkward compared to the crowd that was there. Especially with his nerdy binoculars. Suddenly, a huge devil blows up on the stage. It was red and glowing with flames around it. My eyes grew big and scared. In my 12-year-old mind, a thought occurred to me. As this satanic devil was rising on the stage, I looked inconspicuously to the side with my eye. I said My goodness, My dad is a Satan worshipper. It's funny because when I was growing up, I would tell people this story about my youth and how cool my dad was to have taken me to see ACDC, but he was a Satan worshipper... as a joke. But only to find out in my forties my father is, in fact, a hard-core Luciferian. So, just from these examples, I had as a child with my father Randy Hayes. I knew he was very capable of what I had heard him doing to my grown children. Even though they were adults, I had to protect my children at all costs.

I had started a random conversation with my father and then worked in the fact that I knew he was having sex with my children in the manner of a question. I made a statement of," I know what I have heard." He simply leaned back in his chair and gave me a look as if I was crazy, then a look of surprise upon his face. He never said a word, and I walked away and left it there. I wanted him to be aware I was aware. In the hopes this would deter him from his sexual depravity, he was doing to my children. I never heard these things again in the house. I was left with an uneasiness about how to approach my children with this situation. I looked at them as victims but didn't know how to talk about it with them. I felt very alone in what I had learned about my family because they were all involved with these disgusting acts, and I had no one to turn to who would ever believe me. I was sure my children would have simply denied the facts of the truth, and my grandmother would have probably put me in an insane asylum.

I went on a walk in the woods behind our home a few weeks after this and ran into some rocks stacked up with bob wire wrapped around a big wooden stick and dried blood on it. My instincts told me that this was demonic instantly. Some kind of satanic ritual remanence I had come across accidentally. Then, there was another area with chairs in a circle with rocks around it, like people had been hanging out in the woods behind the house. I just did not think it had to do with my family at all. Until today.

When I started truck driving school,,I was determined to succeed and get away from my family. So, when that didn't work out for me in 2020 due to covid 19. When my father put my things out on the road, I knew it was payback for busting him out about the molestation of my children. Even though I knew this deep down inside, I didn't accept it myself and denied my own reality. Possibly because the pain of truly accepting my own family's dysfunction was too much for me.

CHAPTER 4

THE DARK CARNIVAL AND THEIR GAME
PLAY STUPID GAMES AND GET STUPID PRIZES

After I moved out of Maui's house. I had started getting my unemployment money. Which was helping me out as well. Out of nowhere, I received a letter stating that my funds were being stopped. I had funds still available but was not allowed any further access to my funds. I just assumed that the government was on the up and up and did not question this letter. I simply let it go. I moved into a room I was offered by a client of mine in Oakdale. I was offered another room by someone else at the same time. It was the illusion that I had friends and options. Later, the one that said he has a room too. Never meant it. I needed help later down the road, but he said no. It's all about putting your feet on a rug and then pulling the thing out from under you. This is the enjoyment they delighted in. My pain and my struggles. The game of the dark circus was not fun for me, but they were sure having a great time amid their psychotic mind game. Laughing all the time right in my face. Just cold-hearted evil. I didn't know this, though, because I saw the world through rose colored glasses. All I could say to myself was" I am Interested"! "I am Interested"! What is this? Life was seemingly going fine until I invited someone over. I had a youngster who had been seemingly a dedicated client to me. As a matter of fact, he was the one that I would see every week. I just thought he really liked me. I thought he was sincere in his actions towards his friendship and his loyalty to me as his weekly visits to see me as a client. He was quite a bit younger than me, and it took me a while to feel comfortable with the age difference between us. I was curious about his foot fetish he had. I had never seen such a fetish before. And I didn't mind obliging him in his needs. He made me feel like a Goddess and he knew my worth. I really liked him and thought he was trustworthy. So, I had him come over to see me. I was under the impression that I was an adult and that he was not my boyfriend but my roommate.

He was not happy the next morning with me before leaving the house. I had no clue that he would be so childish and mean. I was looking at buying an R.V. I found that day and put a down payment down on it then had to return to the house to retrieve the rest of the funds I had in my room. On returning to the house, I found the door locks had been changed and there was no answer from him. I was upset by this fact, being that I had all my rent paid up and was being locked out of my room. I contacted the police, who stated that it was not illegal. I was left with my own devices at that moment. I went into the backyard and started to break into my bedroom window. That's when I heard my roommate in the house contacting the police. They showed up after 3 minutes of my actions.

Demanding that I step out from the backyard and begin to explain to me how I was breaking the law. I was devastated by the enforcement of my pertinent behaviors. The law did nothing to stand up for my rights. They did not care about the rental rights I had as a renter. I was being totally disregarded. I was obviously very upset and concerned because I was told oh well. Leave. He locked the door, and it was his house. I needed the rest of the money I had in my room for the R.V. purchase. I put the deposit of 3,000 down on that day. The seller was holding the R.V. for me and expecting me back soon. I ended up leaving the situation and returning to the seller to explain to him how I could no longer purchase his R.V. because of what had happened. The seller had been talking about how he was a man of God and went to church. Said he was a pastor. Took what he had said to heart and that's why I left the 3,000 with him. But he was simply fake to. He used God the father to trick me into relaxing myself around him and his lies he wanted to spew. In order to steal my money, the same day that they already had planned the locks to be change. Back-to-back bombs dropped on me that one day. I mean they never let an opportunity slip by. Not one. They would be in my life a posted up for the plots to be acted out on me. Skits and all. Actors running my days. While I am walking around like everything is semi normal. The way normal people think is day is day people are what they are right. But not in my case these narcissists had complete control of my world right under my nose. Now I know what was so funny to them besides stealing my inheritance. The man with R.V. took my 3,000 dollars deposit. I was devastated to core by the bull crap I was having forced into my wellbeing, but see, these people don't realize how The Most High works. He gives you peace and love when things like that happen. If you have an issue you go to God. I learned don't flip out remain calm, God sees this all and Hes got you. He keep my 3,000 dollars for wasting his time and missing other possible buyers. I did tell him I was going to visit his church and let is congregation know exactly what he had done in such an ungodly manner to me. I was still being a little reactive at this time because I am very strong willed when it comes to being done wrong for no reason. Especially by an individual who said he was about the Lord. That's out… I hate people who use God as front for their crafty deceitful ways. I will call that out any time to your face. I love my Father, and I stick up for him all I can. You can't front on my God like that. Fake people need to be revealed. Especially someone who said hes a pastor. This was just the beginning of the dedicated incompetence of wasted time and money they loved to expel their energy on. If this cult could get me to hurt or cry or waste my time they were doing their job that day. Just nonsense to my eyes. It was so freaky in weird that the hate they would show me didn't even affect me because I am solid in who I am as a person and as a woman. It didn't matter to me because I knew they were doing on purpose. I could say that if these people met me on a different level, they would never have wanted to hurt me the way they were being paid to. In effective abuse. These times only drew me closer to God. I knocked, and he opened the door. He called and I answered. While he was calling of these people, they were hanging up on him. Right in his face. Like nah. I am cool. Shame on them. They were being tested and they all failed.

The police allowed him to go through everything I owned. He had stolen $900.00 cash out of my room, and three days after he had gone through everything and helped himself then, the police allowed me to enter my room. Only then was I told I could take my things out of the garage. I packed my car intricately and quickly and made sure I packed it perfectly so it all fit in one trip. This was to ensure that I did not have to return to my roommate's home. As I was leaving, he came out of his front door ,grabbed a potted plant off his front porch and threw it on my vehicle, scratching my vehicle and almost breaking out the back window. I went to the Oakdale Police Department, and they did not arrest him. They said I could make a citizen's arrest and go to court. At that time, I had never planned on entering a courtroom again, and I didn't want to deal with the drama anymore. So, I then just left the scene. I really did not want to go back to my father's house, so I found a fifth-wheel trailer for free and found a spot at a trailer spot up in Strawberry, California, just a little way up from Twain Harte Ca where my kids lived. I paid for the spot and paid 1,500 dollars to have it moved from Oakdale, Ca. I finally got it put in place and was ready to move into it. It needed the septic hooked up and the electricity to be turned on. I asked my father to come and help me do those things being that he owned his own construction company. He came up to my trailer and refused to help me. He said it was a dump and he wouldn't help me. I could not find anyone that I knew either to help me. I was out of money to have to pay someone to do those things as well. I ended up walking away from my trailer at the park and was forced into moving back to my father's home. Which was the last thing I wanted to do. I had blown 2,400 dollars on trying to be my own person and had failed once again at this attempt. The last thing I wanted to do was to move back to Randy's house.

My daughter had moved into the room I had previously lived in downstairs. So, I ended up moving into the room across from my father's room upstairs. I continued escorting, and as far as I knew, no one knew what I was doing besides my best friend Melisa. I came home one day, and I could hear my father and my son whispering quietly as if they didn't want me to hear what they were talking about. Being a natural-born detective, it perked my curiosity. I then stuck my ear to the crack in the door. I then heard my son say where's the money, my dad stated don't worry, it's in an offshore account in the Canary Islands. Then I heard them whispering to each other something about 25 to life. My intuition immediately told me that they were talking about me. I just knew they were speaking about me. Then I heard Austin ask," where's the money?" My dad then responded, "it's in an offshore account in the Canary Islands. I didn't have a clue about any money and was not sure what they were talking about when it came to this topic. Then, I decided the next day to drive directly to my grandmother's house to inform her of what I had overheard. I arrived at her home and asked her to have a private conversation in her bedroom. I did not want Frank to hear our conversation. I asked her to sit down upon her bed and began to explain the preconceived setup being infiltrated on my life. As I was speaking to her, I believed that I was speaking to a family member who really had my back and loved me. All she had to say was my father would not do something like that to me. He loves me. Basically, I was gaslight by the one person who I believed to be a confidant of mine. She basically brushed off what I had brought to her and dismissed me.

Things just started getting weird and off in my life, but I could never put my finger on it. I just felt the vibes of bad intent being directed towards me. Not only by my family but also by strangers in my communities, from Twain Harte to Modesto. My son even began to call me Shannon and treat me very disrespectfully. This was very frustrating for me and hurt my feelings as well. I would constantly tell him not to call me Shannon. But he just continued to progress in his ugly behavior towards me. I could not understand why my son was treating me so unkindly for no reason. I kept thinking any time my son was going to come into my room and apologize to me for his behavior. I had high hopes that he would come to realize that he was wrong and we would hug and move on passed whatever he had been going through. I was fully prepared to forgive him.

I started to notice strangers while I was staying at the Howard Johnson Hotel were constantly sitting in their cars in front of my room or even just hanging out in direct line of sight when I would open my room door. I get that people sometimes sleep in their cars like that, but it was hours and hours of this, and many times, it was just a regular situation. Something was off with this pattern of behavior. One day,, I was at the hotel sitting outside on my computer when I decided to go back to my room and chill in my bed. It was around 7 in the evening, and the sun had not quite gone down yet. I continued to browse the internet, and that was the last thing I remember. Around 3 A.M., I woke up standing in the shower, the shower running on me. I was fully clothed, shoes and all, with the shower blasting on my new outfit I had just bought. I had no recollection as to what had happened to me from 7 p.m. to 3 a.m. I had experienced missing time for the first time in my life.

I also started noticing there were always ambulances around me. I mean, everywhere I went, there would be an ambulance parked. I felt as if they were waiting for me to commit suicide and they were going to grab up my body and no one would even know I where I was. Once again my intuition. I also started to notice a lot of satellites following me around as well as drones too. My bedroom faced the Stanislaus National Forest, and I would see these very bright lights that would float from side to side. I simply thought it was people camping. I would get my flashlight and shine it back to them. It was like a game I was playing. This would happen often. I received a text message from an unknown man with a picture attached of me on my porch and it said 'hey babe what are you doing?' also noticed that drones were flying around my dads house as well. I am very aware of my surroundings, and I always have been. and I have never in my life seen so many low flying satellites and drones.

On my way back from Turlock to Sonora I took the back way home through a little town called Snelling. On my way I decided to pull over and use the phone. As I was sitting there on the side of the road minding my own business. When all sudden a huge military government Black Hawk style helicopter came flying over me with the door wide open. I could see inside the helicopter. It was full of both military and suits. They were all staring, pointing and laughing at me. The helicopter continued. To go over the field across from me. They went back and forth about four times. Ensuring that I would see them. At one point they flew away and then came back. Alright, this point. I had gotten out my cell phone and started to record it but telling myself I will never show anyone this video, I will look completely crazy. This is actually the first time I've spoken of it as well. This was the time I realized the government was part of what was happening to me, not just my family and not just my community. This was bigger than me. A few weeks after this I had ran into my friend Jason who worked. At Sierra Conservation Center as the Lieutenant. I began to tell him the outrageous story of what had been happening to me. And he had stated, Shannon, be careful out here. I heard the other officers at work talking about what's happening to you. And people die in this program, so be careful. My ears couldn't believe what I was hearing. And how he disregarded the help I was asking for. It seemed as if everywhere I turned for help, I would get turned away or shut down. I had no one to turn to. No friends, no family, no law enforcement. And I knew if I had spoken to a therapist or a counselor about it, it would have been lights out for me. Jason. OK. Another odd thing that had begun happening was that I noticed everybody around me started purchasing nice vehicles, homes. And clothing. I never felt jealous or envious of these items and purchases. I just was wondering how they are affording all of this extravagant lifestyle? My best friend Melissa was in no need of funds. Then we to she even invited to her a wedding she was having that she had said it cost $10,000 and her ring was $10,000. This came from a girl who grew up on welfare and her parents never went to college or tried to do anything with their lives. I could not comprehend how she could afford these things. She even went as far as had braces put on and a brand new set of breasts that she had fixed.

I had a client I was seeing that worked and lived at the fish hatchery close to Sonora. He was a giant man with a kind heart. We would have deep conversations about life. He had shared with me how he would help a friend of his out with a group of people that help people and save them from cults. I thought, wow, that's great. I did not know that I was one of those people. I had up and moved suddenly after sharing that with him, and I never spoke to him again. After I had awakened to my truth, I would often think about this man and how he knew when he met me who I was, and he was part of my secret helpers.

I was staying at the Days Inn in Modesto. I was put into a room that had a generator running next door. I called the front desk to complain about the noise and even asked them to come listen to what I had been dealing with. The woman came into my room and said it was not that bad, but then she said she would move me. She proceeded to move me into another room that was down the hall. And I couldn't believe it when another generator started up in the next room to me. I then heard I heard the leaf blower out in the front, so I took turned on the record button. As I looked down the stairs with my video camera rolling on my phone, I could see two men standing at the end of the staircase. With two leaf blowers blowing, and, they weren't even blowing anything. They were just standing there with the loud noise blowing out of their machines, which I have on video to this day. This was something that occurred everywhere I went, every day, nonstop, 24 hours a day, seven days a week. Without a break in between. As I'm writing this to you, I'm still dealing with a few of the noise harassments, which is insane. Insane because the game is no longer a game, and it is over. They just won't let it go. It seems that they don't know anything else to do with their lives. It's quite sad. It's quite sad.

I was concerned for my safety and decided to go to the Turlock Police Department and make a report in case something happened to me. I sat in an interview room with a female officer and described all the incidents that I was concerned for my life in detail. I explained to her I only made the report because I am a single woman, and I felt I needed help. She laid back in her chair and simply said, "Well, it can't be everyone"! I stuck up for myself and said, "That's not what I said, that is what's you said". She basically acted as if I was overreacting and then put words in my mouth that I had not said. When I walked out of the police station, I felt as if I was tossed aside, as if I was undeserving of being taken seriously. Authorities who are civil servants of the public. They are the ones that are supposed to protect and serve people in need of help. But who do you go to when they are the same authorities who were creating harm to people?

One morning, I was cooking breakfast with my

daughter Hannah. As I was making the bacon, I could see out the side of my eye that Hannah was making some aggressive hand gestures and saying something. I couldn't quite hear what she had said with it. So, I quickly turned around and asked her what she had said. She replied," that life right there, I am going to need that"! I was getting a bad vibe from her comment and became upset with her, stating I don't know what that means. I am your mother, so don't ever talk to me like that again. I asked her where she heard that from, and she said it was a post from Facebook. I didn't know that she really meant what she said at the time. It didn't make sense at the time to me, but I know now that she was not on my side.

I had an issue with my storage unit company and had to move my things out immediately because I had too many locks on my unit. They also had removed the original lady that I had a good relationship with at the storage business. One day, she was there, then the next, she was gone. I found that odd but didn't want to argue with the new individuals that were now harassing me, so I moved all my things to my father's house with his permission. I had put all the boxes and items up in the loft area of his home. I had been visiting a friend's home one evening and was in a great mood when I arrived home. I arrived home to pick up my make up bag and was going to head to see another friend in Modesto. I opened the door to my bedroom but couldn't open the door at all. It was blocked by all the boxes and items I had brought from my storage unit. My entire room was packed full, piled on my bed and everything. I became upset and yelled in my father's room about why this had happened. He acted as if he knew nothing about it. I knew that was ridiculous because his room was directly across from mine. My son then came barreling upstairs like a tyrant. He got into my face and started yelling at me viciously and became very volatile. I was so confused as to what was happening because I had done nothing to deserve such treatment. My son then punched me right in the mouth and made me bleed. I grabbed my face in shock and began to cry. My father had witnessed the entire scene and did nothing. I grabbed my purse and my keys and ran down the stairs. As I was leaving the house, I heard them saying that they were calling the police on me. I got in my car and turned around in our very small, unlighted cul-de-sac. I was so upset and nervous at the time when I hit the side of my daughter's vehicle and didn't even realize what I hit. I thought it was a garbage can. I did not intend to hit her car.

I ended up driving into Sonora. When I got off the freeway, I saw one of the ambulances that I was seeing around and felt a little angry as it passed by me. I then pulled into the parking lot to the Wendys to gather myself together. I simply couldn't understand what had just happened. That's when I recalled the conversation that I had overheard about 25 to life and then realized that this was what was happening to me. I was being set up by my own blood for no reason. That's when a police car pulled right behind me, and an officer approached my car. He asked me to get out of the car and placed me under arrest. As he placed me into the back of the cop car, I saw an older gentleman pull up in a little Toyota truck and to start talking to the other officers that had shown up at the scene. I was in the back of the cop car for an hour or so as the officers and the strange man had a discussion about me. I could tell they were talking about me because they were pointing in my direction. I even asked one policeman who that man was, but there was no reply. I was then taken to the jail and booked on felony charges of terrorist threats against my son along with assault. My son had stated to the police that I had threatened his life and punched him in the mouth. Lies were placed on me without question to my side of the story. The charges held a sentence of 25 to life term. The setup had been committed that I had told my grandmother about a month prior. I was in jail for 7 days, then bailed out with my covid funds. I went directly to Wendys to see if my car was still there and was surprised to see it was. I assumed it would have gotten towed away. I didn't have my keys to my car and was hoping the police had left my keys on my floorboard, but they were nowhere to be found. I contacted the police station and was told my keys had been placed into evidence. I was unable to get my keys due to the person in charge of the evidence being on vacation. I called a client of mine to come pick me up. I got a ride back to Sonora three days later and was able to finally get my keys and my car. I had a restraining order placed upon me from going to my father's home, but needed to retrieve my things from my bedroom. I contacted my father by phone and asked when I could come pick up my stuff and was given a time to come. When I showed up to the house and entered my room, I walked into a completely empty room. All my things had been removed from the house without any explanation. Not one of them would take responsibility for the thief that had occurred.

I went to the police station, made a report and asked the police to contact my father about getting my things back. The police were told my things were there, and I was more than welcome to come pick it up. I was given the run around for weeks. The police did not want to do anything about the thief, which was crazy to me. No arrests or anything. Finally, my father met up with me, and I received my laptop, a few pairs of sweatshirts, and some junk clothes. I was tossed out in the cold and turned away from my entire family at this point. It seemed to be that, for some odd reason, I had been shunned by my close friends and family all at once for no good reason.

CHAPTER 5
FRIENEMIES

I had a few close friends growing up. My best friend Melisa, I had known since I was seven years old. My mother had married her uncle and we became friends even though she was three years older than me. I only chose to call her the one true best friend of my life. We shared everything about our life experiences growing up. The births of our children, birthday parties, holidays and trips were major life events that I thought had brought us close. She was the only one I would tell things to in confidence. I noticed that she would never answer her phone when I called her, but when I would visit her house, she would constantly answer her phone. She would even ignore me and talk for hours to other people while I was there. I started to feel like she was doing it on purpose and began to pull away from her more and more. When I started escorting, I even told her what I was doing, even though she thought I was gross for it. As the gang stalking started happening to me, she was the first one I told what I was experiencing. Thinking I could trust her at the time.

She said maybe it's God doing it to you. I didn't believe that for one minute when she said that. But knowing she has always been in the occult secrets, she knew exactly what my soul was getting ready to go through. My destiny, she was trying to swap with me. I had no clue my own best friend was secretly hating on me and was involved in trying to unalive me.

The gang stalking began to become evident to me as the days went by. I was living in my car because no one would allow me to stay with them, not even Melisa. I couldn't believe that even my best friend Melisa had turned her back on me in my time of need when, years previously, I had allowed her and her children to live with me and my kids when she had nowhere to live. With nowhere to go, I decided to go camping at Woodward Lake and set up a tent for the weekend. The first night, the wind kicked up in Oakdale, Ca. which is not the norm for this area. It was blowing around 50 miles per hr. It was so bad it twisted my tent up and almost blew away many times. I noticed the gang stalkers around me flashing their lights and revving car engines while chilling camping that weekend. I was kind of freaking out. I couldn't understand what was happening, but I was interested in what was going on and began to be super sensitive to my surroundings. I stood also on the shore and noticed a group of men standing across from me, just staring and pointing at me. I knew they were a part of what was happening to me. I intuitively felt as if witches were causing this weather all weekend long. But I quickly rejected this thought because I did not even believe in witches at this time. It's so funny, though, how that thought came into my mind and tried to get me to hurt myself with their torment and stalking. Then I saw search and rescue boats all around me there, as if they were waiting for me to drown myself at the lake. I left the lake and went to Perkos to eat. While I was waiting for a table, I overheard this group of men sitting at the counter talking about the search and rescue at the lake. It was odd to hear them discussing this, and I feel they were part of it, too. My intuition has always been on point, and I know this now.

I had gone to school with a kid named Christian Blum, and over the years, we would get together and party together but we never dated. Our relationship was purely a sexual connection. Nothing more, nothing less. But I started to see some weird things happening to me around 2020 and felt I could talk to Christian about the evil things I was seeing. I told him how I would drive around and see conveys of the same-colored cars, the people driving looked directly at me with creepy, evil, demonic smiles upon all their faces as they passed by me. I knew I was seeing demons face to face. It was crazy for me to see, but I knew I was not crazy in my head. What I was experiencing was happening to me, and the things I would get back to research were always what crazy people think. Over and over, God was giving me the topics to look up, and I could not accept these crazy resolutions. So, I would just push it out of my mind, almost as if I were vomiting it out as false information even though it was happening to me. I started researching Secret societies, necromancy, the MK Ultra program, mind control, and alchemy and listening to lyrics in songs that led me down other rabbit holes of my mind. I was diving deep into the aspects of these secret societies and what they believed. The documentaries and youtube videos I would come across were indeed full of nuggets of things to research, which led me to find factual proof to tie it back to the original information. It was like my mind was a tree, and it was just growing branch after branch as I connected the dots to all the different but same information. The one same occurrence in it all is love and giving it over to a higher power. I found documentaries on Tubi to be very helpful. The information I was finding was starting to validate that my life experience was real. It was, without a doubt, a true portion of our unknown reality. Only these are subjects and topics no one knows or would even believe are happening to me. Every word I say is true and is going to be hard for some people to believe. I am not here to make them believe I am here to share a message. A message of faith and hope and glory to God. I would tell Christian about the convoys of cars all the same colors or the same type. It was always an obvious pattern. The one thing that was freaking me out was the people wouldn't look like people at all. Their faces were contorted,, and their wicked smiles were pure evil. As each one would pass by, they would not be looking forward but right at me with that creepy demon smile. They didn't even look human anymore. Christian acted as if he didn't hear me when I was reaching out. Left me feeling ignored. He sat me down at his computer one night and had me watch a movie called Zeitgeist. This side of him I had never seen, and it made me realize that he was kind of a deep thinker. Which is not a characteristic I had ever seen of him. I had told him I was escorting, and sometimes he would come to see me at the hotel room I would stay in. It was almost like when he found out I was escorting, he had started to call me more and more to hang out. When I was trying to work and make my money, he was simply trying to distract me from progressing, though.

He told me one day while visiting him. Because I was talking about it again he stated, "It doesn't even matter to . You'll be dead in 8 months anyway," and he wasn't going to unplug me from the matrix. I had the insight to say back to him, 'Maybe I won't unplug you'. The statement that I would be dead in eight months only gave me the motivation to march strongly ahead in my mission of exposing what was happening. Exposing it not to my own mind but to the whole world. He was not hanging out with me because he was my friend or friend with benefits, was a job at this point. He was a paid actor for the gov. agents to infiltrate my personal life. It is such an unbelievable thing to realize. How would evil plot and plan to this extent. I had no clue that he was a part of a secret society in any way, shape or form until he made hurtful statements about my life. Christian told me he was heading overseas to Paris. I was like, what the heck? He had never left Turlock since I had known him. But I was so trusting I just assumed that he went there for personal reasons and didn't ask questions. Today, though, I know he was going there to pay practitioners to do spell work on me. God told me he was going to take the evil intended for me and make it for my good. This cult was out to murder me, and spells are not cheap either. They cost a lot of money to do. No weapon formed against me shall proper.

So, then I began to investigate and ask questions every time I saw him. He then told me a few months later, I was at his house, and I was asking questions. That was the day he had told me that "I was the key"! I knew at this moment that this was bigger than me, and it was spiritual. He told me they can read our minds and see through buildings without equipment of any kind, just with the naked eye. Also, can see in the dark, built in night vision. In October of 2021, he was dating a woman who he seemed to really like a lot. Which was cool, I had never seen him in love before. It was almost as if he was under a spell; I had thought about it. Just like a puppy dog following her around and bowing down to her demands. Buying her all-new wardrobe and wigs and shoes. Who was I to say anything if my so-called friend was happy? We had been parting at his home together, and I left my purse unattended, not thinking I had to worry about my personal items like my phone would be stolen from my purse blatantly. I knew one of them had taken it because when I noticed it was gone, I turned on a phone that was used strictly for internet and went to google to find my device. The whole time I was trying to contact my phone, I never let on that I was aware my phone was gone. Find my device located my phone, and it was directly still in his house somewhere. It had been located without a doubt. I had to suck up what they had done and never mentioned it. Then, the next time I was there, she told me that, yes, she had gone through my phone and my phone numbers. I didn't even ask her this. She volunteered to give this information to me. But I was so dazed and confused from all the stalking and harassment that day it didn't hit me what she had done until 3 days later. As I realized, wow my friends went through my phone, which is something I would never even fathom doing to either of them. That's weird to me. I would have no reason to go behind their backs to be sneaky. A few weeks before Halloween, they both invited me to a big, fancy Halloween costume party. They said lots of people would be there and had already started putting up these extravagant decorations inside and outside of his home. I had not been escorting as much due to the community abuse stalking that happened to me, and I was living in my car. God had given me the warning not to attend the party. He said stay right here in your car, baby, turn your phone off. You don't need to be anywhere around that house. Bad vibes all around. Christian's girlfriend Carol ended up passing away in 2022. She moved away, and got clean and had a brain aneurysm on her way to a job one morning soon after this discovery of mine.

Another time that occurred with him was when he started writhing around on the bed as if he was being possessed or in some sort of seizure for about 20 min. It was so long that I began to wonder if I should be concerned or if I should laugh at this point. He then stood up with his arms out wide and his back to me, and he stated," I am 4,000" years old," so hearing this comment, I came back with 'Oh, yeah"! Then he said, "I am 4,000 years old, and I run everything, even you!". My response was, "You don't run me!" He said yes, even you! I do run you". I laughed under my breath and told him you will never run me. I got my purse, grabbed my keys and left thinking, wowsa what in God's good name just happened in there? I felt the evil exuding out of him in every way. Then, about a month later after this incident, I met another person named Justin Roberts in Columbia, CA. which is a few hours from Turlock, CA. I met him walking down the street, and he invited me over to his home that evening. As we were visiting, he made a statement 'Don't you remember who you are?" I had no idea what he was getting at" and was concerned that his mental state was a little off. He also asked me if I remembered being Izzy. I began to ponder that name through my mind and could not come up with any memory whatsoever of this name or anything that would conjure up a thought about leading me to find this Izzy person he claimed I was. He then said the next sentence that blew my mind. He said, "I am 2,000 years old' I was sitting in a computer chair of his and turned it towards the wall and asked the wall, "wtf". I was tripping out! Christian stated that he was 4,000 years old, and Justin said that he was 2,000 years old. I couldn't wait to go tell Christian that I was seeing a younger man. This man also told me how he had a band and had his music on youtube music. His band's name was 27 inch pipe. He played some of his music, and his lyrics were very descriptive of how gang stalkers move. I was well aware he was part of this group. He was crazy too, he would talk to 6 different people that weren't even there. I was so freaked out by his behavior that I walked out of his room and knocked on his roommates door to ask them," is he really like that, or is he messing with me"? They told me no he's really like that! I had stopped by his house one night, and he had pulled his penis out. I told him I wasn't going to sleep with him. He did not get mad or anything. He just masturbated the hole time I was there. While he was masturbating he had also turned on the news and put it in slow motion. He told me that the news lady was trying to show him her vagina and I said how. He rewound the newsreel and played it back in slow motion and was describing to me how she was opening her legs the way she was for him to look at her vagina. I was like, wowsa this guys out of his mind. Another thing he asked me was if I felt him having sex with me the night before. He said he had sex with me through telepathy. I had been alone in my bed asleep the night before and did not feel anything. I boldly told him no, I did not feel you. He seemed shocked that I did not understand what he was talking about. He seemed to know who I was even though I did not. I was only to continue to hang out with him at this point only for investigative purposes. He had called me and asked me to come over. When I got to his house, he had another woman there. She was having a basic conversation with me and seemed normal, but things turned, and she tried to start a physical fight with me. I was feeling set up by him. I did not allow her to get me to act out of character for anyone. I grabbed my purse and walked out the door. That was the last time I went to his house or spoke to him. I knew he was looking to get me in trouble and was not going to allow him or her to win.

This part of my story is about the massive amount of patronization and mind fragmentation that was being done to me by this cult. They did so many awful things to me daily and did not stop for years. The insurmountable amount of incidents would make this book very long. There are so many things I can't even remember the full totality of them. I decided to just make a list of the things and behaviors they did. You're going to say to yourself, after you read the list, well, these are all normal things you see in the world going on. I am aware that they are all basic situations and behaviors humans do. But when these things begin happening to you daily over and over and over many times. It is not normal. It starts to become a form of trauma and stress to the mind. I have done research on how this will break a human mind and turn you crazy. They used these tactics along with isolating me from friends and family to work in unison. As I had nowhere to live, no one to turn to or no one to help me. They have you in their sick, depraved game of trauma and human torture. Plus, if you start telling others that cars are following me, people are following me, and people are jingling their keys loudly by me all the time. That is the setup for your destruction because the statements will make you sound out of your mind or schizophrenic, and you'll be locked away and marked legally loony and placed in padded room. I would often find my family's items at client's homes, such as a pillowcase that matched my father's comforter in his home. It was not a design that was sold at Walmart or anything. My friend Melisa had this torn computer chair for years. I had seen that chair over and over so many times that when I saw it at one of the clients' homes in the garage, it wasn't hard to see that they were trying to gaslight me in this manner with items. That same client even has a rug she did have in her home, along with a kitchen nook table and bench set. Hers some more weird things they would do. I would go to a store, and strangers would always stand right behind me as I would be purchasing things. They would be right in my personal space. Loud helicopters and loud airplanes fly directly over me and even in circles sometimes. At the hotels the maid carts would always be at my door every time I would be there, false arrests constantly, ambulances and fire trucks driving by me constantly, strangers driving by and honking daily no matter where I would be, any time I would go through a drive through restaurant I would be there for 30 or 40 min, city buses would go by and the bus would make a laughing sound, strangers standing in my way blocking me and laughing at me everywhere I went, dogs barking constantly, loud garbage trucks would pull up and bang cans around, lawn mower and weed eaters were always going in my vicinity, generators going, vacuums on loud cars roaring by me revving up their engines, strangers swarming me in cars laughing and flipping me off, banging on the walls of the hotels I would stay at, cars with one headlight or one hub cap removed, vehicles pulled to the side of the road with flashers going all ailing the roads I would drive on, cars with one headlight, cars flashing there brights at me, cars trying to run me off the road, people wearing plaid clothing, they used dollies and carts a lot, entering my hotel rooms when I was gone and breaking my Bluetooth speaker charge connection on multiple speakers I kept buying, stealing my things, vandalizing my car, diesel trucks left running loudly, phone and emails was hacked took hours to make profiles or get verified for apps I would want to use, children purposely walking in my way blocking isles multiple times in one store visit, so you react and yell at a child and they get you out of character by yelling at a child. I never fell for it. I simply transmuted the energy directed towards me by thinking of how they were going to get caught over and over and over, as well as saying it out loud with my mouth.

In my research, I began to notice a lot of news stories being broadcasted about adults assaulting kids by actually punching youngsters in these stores. Right when I saw what had been videoed, I saw why it happened, but whether anybody else would see it too was my dilemma.I knew why these little kids were getting punched. It took a lot of positive thinking as well as endless patients on the daily, lots of patience.. This cult trains their children on how to be annoying and how to behave in distasteful behavior on purpose. They would instead prefer to teach their children how to harm another person, be it an adult or child when they need to teach them how you treat others so your life will be. They are taught how to make sure they annoy adults at the requests of the parents. I began to connect the dots as to all the school shooting that started to happen. I realized that this cult is teaching their children to bully adults so if they are doing it to adults surely they are going to school and creating chaos and abuse to other students. You would never think that there are people purposely teaching children to drive other chil-dren to the point of snapping out and shooting others in their school. It's like poking a bear over and over, and when the bear attacks them, they blame the bear. One time, I was driving down the road, and this group of people threw something at my car, and I pulled over to confront the criminals and called the police. I began to record these individuals while waiting for the police. The woman that was part of the group stated to me at least I have a job, which was mind-blowing that this woman knew that about me. The police came and did nothing about the felony committed against me. The police showed up and went to speak to them first. Then came over to ask me my side. I told them the story, and they simply said it is not against the law to throw things at cars. I was well aware that it's most definitely a felonious crime to throw anything at a moving vehicle. Once again, I was let down by the people who had taken an oath to protect and serve the public.

All these people in my community were doing these things to me was freaking me out, and I started to talk to God more and more. I was taught at church that chaos and confusion only come from the devil, and I was not going to allow these evil people to change who I was. I started to talk to my family members about what was happening to me. My mother was living in Hilmar with my brother Joe Lair and his wife, Kim. My brother had children, and Kim had her children. They were also raising one of my sister's children, so it was to see my nieces and nephews when I would go visit. I never said I had mentioned anything to my brother or Kim, only my mother. I told her that I was being followed by people and the police. It was funny because we had been sitting on the porch when I was telling her this, and a few police cars drove by the house. When I saw the cars, I told my mother, "see, there they are now," and she just looked at me like I was out of my mind. Over the years, I kept talking to her about it but was left feeling helpless and made to feel I was not mentally well. I knew darn well ,that I was not crazy and that I had all my marbles. Even though no one wanted to listen to me, I kept telling them my truth. One day, I went to visit my mother in Hilmar and found my brother's house empty. They packed their things and moved without mentioning a word to me. They even changed their phone number. I felt hurt by their actions. I eventually found out where my mother was living in Turlock, but I never saw my brother or Kim again. About 2 years later, I was walking up to a liquor store called Pop and Cork in Turlock. As I was walking into the store, I noticed Kim getting out of their car and my brother in the driver's seat. I felt like they had ditched out on me when they moved and changed their phone number, so I was not going to give them my attention. I stared straight ahead as if they were invisible. When I came out of the store, I locked eyes with my brother and then looked away pretending to not care he was there. I didn't say a word when suddenly, I heard him yell loudly for everyone in the parking lot to hear," You're crazy, you don't know what you're talking about, it's all in your mind". I turned around and flipped him off. I had never said anything to him about what I was going through, so it was odd for him to speak about it. I was not going to argue my case or fight with him as he had hoped by making his comment. I proceeded to walk down the street, but when they passed by me in their car, they both were screaming, "You're insane, and you needed mental help". That was the day I realized my brother and his wife were also involved in what was happening to me.

Another family member I had decided to reach out to was my grandmother. I went to my grandmother's house one afternoon and spoke with her about the stalking and things that were happening to me. She only said to me, "Who has the money to do that to you? And who would do this to you? You are just a broke girl!" I also complained to her about how Austin and my father had stolen my 500.00 mirror! Her response was, "why would you buy something that expensive?" as if the thief was warranted because I don't deserve to purchase nice things. I was clueless as to who or what was doing this to my life and once again felt dismissed by my family.

I left my grandmother's house that day and went the side country way back to the valley. I had passed by a sign out on the road that said trailers for sale. I figured I might find something and pulled into the driveway. I introduced myself and found them to be very kind. They were a nice older couple, Jeannie and Micheal. They invited me to stay in a little trailer for rent on their property. I really liked the woman; she was kind to me and played her fake role as if she were a true actress. She really fooled me. I ended up finding out a lot about these people just by observing Jeannie. I started to talk about the stalking that was happening to me. Jeannie also opened my eyes to the fact these people were not people. They wear something she called a meat suit. A meat suit sounded like a creature wearing a human body. She told me that it had happened to her in the past, too. I never knew anyone who could even get on my level about my situation till then. She told me it was called Gang stalking. I thought she was a little crazy because she told me it was my family doing it to me, which I did not believe for one min. I did not even look up or google gang stalking for three months or so. Once I looked it up the flood gates opened to more and more things to research. More targeted individuals like me. Jeannie had told me something about gang stalking, and I thought that she had to be part of it. Because what I saw when I looked at it was exactly that, gang stalking. But how! You would not think in a million years that she would know my family. I met her by random chance. I drove by a sign outside of her house and pulled into the driveway. Now, my own mind started to rationalize that fact. How could all these strangers know each other. It just seemed impossible to me. And make the situation to happen for me to meet Jeannie and Mike on purpose. Or at least under their illusions.

I was then determined to keep on researching things God had started to direct me to look up online. I was getting download after download. There was another man renting an R.V. on Jeannie's property, too. This guy always had a loud dirt bike going, constantly revving it up. Day or night. I did not realize at the time it was part of the noise harassment level one beginners. I did not connect this with the gang stalking at the time. I began to think things were off with her, and I felt like she was reading my mind and stalking me as well. For example is, I went to Atwater to see Mark, the one faithful love bomber client; I would see him every weekend. Jeannie lived in Jamestown, which was far away from Atwater. I drove to his house and back that same night. The next morning, she had made a statement to me, "You looked ridiculous on top of him last night." I was tripping out on her statement. That meant she had to have been watching me somehow. I then wanted to test my theory that she could read my mind, so I started texting horrible things in a fake message and was sitting far away from her, and she began pacing back and forth and getting upset out of nowhere when I began typing things about her. She got irritated and asked me to leave her house. I did and went out to my trailer. I knew she was reading my mind after the test I did on her. The next day, I was invited to go to my friend Melisa's wedding, and I got dressed to go. I drove to Atwater and was going to go to the wedding. As I pulled up, I saw a bunch of people I didn't recognize at all, and they were standing outside of their cars and staring right at me as if they had been waiting for me to show up. I decided not to even stop and kept on going by. I got the feeling I shouldn't attend the wedding and decided to drive back to Jamestown. God was giving me the warning of bad people once again. It was not safe for me to be around the people that I had trusted my entire life. Not safe at all and I am so thankful I had the guidance of my spirit guides and the Lord to show me what these people were doing. God saw all the things I was not seeing and made sure in many ways to alert me to the betrayals going on behind my back.

I was not comfortable staying at the trailer after figuring out she was reading my mind and spying on me. Plus, I had gone into her husband's house and saw symbols written on the ceiling of the home. It was very satanic in my eyes. I was driving out by Oakdale, CA, in the country when I saw a fifth-wheel trailer for sale and contacted the owner to inquire about the price. I had gone to meet him and look at the trailer, and while there, I gave him a little rundown of my story and situation. He completely blew my mind and told me he was giving me the trailer for free. I felt so blessed and excited to have this offer. I immediately contacted a trailer spot in Strawberry, Ca. I paid the credit check fee, filled out the application and paid in full for my trailer space. I then paid 1,500 to get the trailer towed from Oakdale to Strawberry, CA, which was right up the hill from my children, who were still living at my father's in Twain Harte, Ca. I was so excited to have my own spot and had been planning on how to decorate my yard and the vibe for my porch. I just needed someone to fix the toilet pump tubes that were rotten. I also needed a 220-watt cable cord for the electricity to be turned on. I could not get my father or anyone to fix anything on my trailer. He just showed up, walked around and called it a piece of shit. And how it would be a waste of time for him to work on it. I could not find anyone I called to help me either. I had gotten a phone call from my grandmother, and she told me that my son moved out of my father's house and that my father was going to be getting back with his ex-wife. They had been divorced for around 13 years or so. I was glad to hear he had her back in his life. I decided to contact my father and asked if I could come back. I ended up abandoning the trailer at the park because no one would help me fix anything, and the people at the park were even rude and mean to me. He said yes, so I packed up my things quickly and left the trailer park immediately without saying a word to park management. My father's ex-wife Susan was living at the house now, but we had been getting along fine to times we had run into each other at the house. I thought, cool. I'll let all the pasts go with the things she had done and be an adult. I wanted to show I could have a real relationship with my stepmother. No fakeness or ill intentions coming from my side. We had been talking to one another, and she had made a statement about how she used to hang around Satan worshippers and stories that happened too. I was being told these stories as she was holding a bible in her hands in my father's porch balcony. I thought, wow, maybe she's changed and really is about God today and began to give her the benefit of the doubt.

As time went by, I started seeing the things that Austin and my father had stolen from me. All my things started popping up around the house. Susan was wearing my clothes and sunglasses right in front of me. I began to silently collect my things without saying a word and put them back in my room. One day, I put one of my shirts in my room, and Susan tried to fight me. I had to close my bedroom door on her to stop her from hitting me. I knew what my family members were up to, and I wasn't going to let them score any points off me on their pursuit of lame setup. They were placing my things around the house so I would see them, and it would start a fight. They thought I would react like the old me. Impulsive, violent, loud and argumentative. No, this time, I was the bigger person. I took the high road, and they couldn't understand it. Susan was not even sleeping in the bed with my father and had placed a mattress on the ground right at the entrance of their room. The placement of her bed put her right outside my bedroom. She would be sitting right there outside the door all the time. Creep. I thought she was odd for doing that and began to see a similarity to gang stalking. I had gotten up to use the bathroom and used the one in their room. Usually, I would go to the bathroom downstairs, but it was 5 a.m., and I almost didn't make it to the bathroom. I had caught Susan by surprise. I caught her watching gang-stalking videos on YouTube. That is when I realized that she and my father were aware of what was happening to me. I could not deny it anymore.

I started obtaining new clients to see in the Bay area and began going to the city because I was making better money over there. This is when strangers began to run me off the highway all the time. It was happening so much I knew it was not just a fluke. Also, my map quest would always go haywire and stop working. I would be over in San Fransico and not have a clue as to how to get where I had clients waiting on me. This would cause me to be late or sometimes not find the place at all. I made myself self-look stupid and lost out on money many times when they played games with my map quest. to go to make my money. I would get so frustrated. This was how I knew this was much bigger than me. They had control of my phone and emails. My mail was even compromised and held from me multiple times. On overnight stay in Hayward. I was staying at a hotel and was feeling my Spidey senses perking up. That day, I had really been attacked and delayed. With so much happening to me that day, I decided to go around the parking lot to write down makes and models with license plates. I had started doing this a lot. I almost got obsessed with writing down cars license and descriptions. Once I did match a car to two different towns, it had followed me. I had become obsessed with doing this constantly. But as I stepped out of my car, I put it in the park and pulled the emergency brake. I stepped around the side of an SUV to get a good look at their license numbers when suddenly, my headlights were moving backward. I realized my car was no longer parked. I assumed some little punks were stealing my car. I approached my car quickly but not fast enough to stop it from the door, snapping backward as it hit another car in the parking lot. It then continued to roll straight into one more vehicle. I was so nervous that I would get in trouble and entered my car, put it in gear and proceeded to drive away. Now that my door was snapped back and wouldn't shut, it was hard to drive. I pulled out of the hotel and checked out the damage. I had to find someone to bang out the bend in the door and had to place a gate lock the outside to shut it. This was awful and really destroyed my vehicle. This was another example of the sneaky and ruthless acts there were done to me. They would partake in acts of destruction any opportunity they could get. When it happened to me, I knew I had put my break on without a doubt, but I still questioned myself. Gas lights me. That is why they do those types of things is: to make you question your own mind and, therefore, create self-doubt.

As the months of random harassment and distorted beliefs of my own reality went by. It was prominent to me that my clients had all begun to try to talk me into lowering my service rate. I have always known my self-worth and rarely would allow that. I simply could not believe how it seemed to be all of them more and more day by day. If I were not so enlightened, I wouldn't have caught this pattern of trying to break me down. But I never would have expect less than who I am. I would loudly declare aloud that this evil will not conquer, and it is already written that you all lose. The meek shall inherit the world, not evil. I would also say I do not know why you think you are going to get away with this. I know you are going to get caught one of these days, and I am going to have the last laugh in the end! Just watch and see. I sometimes would walk right up to them sitting in their cars and boldly state these predictions to them. Only to be met with laughter and denial of my confidence. I would sometimes say crazy things like this to these strangers in hopes I would be met with a confused face or, wow, what a weirdo smirk. I was hoping someone would ask me what I was talking about. That was never the case. Everyone always came back with a response to my threats of vindication. Once, I had told these men at a gas station 'I am so glad that I can give you a pay check," and they responded, 'Thank you".

Riding the bus one afternoon, a stalker sat right by me and asked if I knew anything about myself. And of course, I had no clue as to what he was talking about, but I didn't want him to know this fact. So, my response was yes, of course I do. Good, he said, that's good. I decided to ask him, "So what did they tell you to do me?" and He said, 'Well, they gave me tazer because they said you can get a little wild sometimes." And that I should take you if you get out of control. I was shocked was that this man had just said he had been sent to taze you. I took this as my shot to get off the bus, only to have the man follow me as I walked away, telling me how awful my outfit was and how ugly my hair was. Telling me to ask the electric company guys chilling in their truck if they wanted to have sex with me. I told him to get away and just ignored him. I then just wanted to exit the scene they wanted to create. I ignored the harassment. The only way I could block out these situations most of the time was to not give in to what I knew they wanted from me. I knew they wanted me to fight back with words or to get physical, but I felt more empowered by simply turning the tables on them. God would always let me know how much more powerful I was than them, and I stood firmly in killing them with kindness. They simply couldn't comprehend what I was doing to them. They had never had someone not indulge in toxic games. Most people react instantly by yelling at them or even getting violent within them, which then, they get to become the victim even though they were the bully you to begin with. It' was the most childish behavior coming from grown people. I used to feel like I was babysitting an entire community of toddlers.

One particular new client I met up with at a park in Modesto in a local park community one really blew my mind. I met up with him at a local private park at around 11 p.m., and we walked to the playground to have our session. I looked around and noticed that there were four matching tents set up in different areas of the park amongst the trees. Posted perfectly set up. Identical tents were set up as if waiting for the show. Me being me. I knew that people were watching. I had no idea how real this was. Never thinking of the Illuminati. My client's name was Tim from Merced. He was always very violent and aggressive with me. He was a Freemans and involved with the illuminate. He was part of watching me, and recording me from the first meeting. This group continued to watch me and follow me and my sexual escapades all these years. Illegally obtaining videos of me without my permission. With him and many other people I was with. I knew they wanted me to be part of something more than I could understand, but I wanted nothing to do with it, and

I almost died because I wasn't about being like them. How could someone currently be directed toward Satan and thinking that I would be ok with it? I know God was with me and will never forsake me this entire time. He let me know that these people wanted to ruin my life before I even got to live it. My intuition is on point, and I never ignore this very helpful gift the Lord gave me. This is how God saved me from this cult over and over again.

CHAPTER 6

I SAW THE SIGN

I had been driving out in the back forty on Highway J59. ,It was on a mountainous road that was made for horseback riding trails and day use. It was dusty and in the outs. I was homeless and needed a spot to not be bothered, so I rolled up on the side of the road to rest and smoke a joint. Remember, my car door didn't shut at all, it only stayed shut with the gate latch shut all the way. I had to use the restroom and relieve myself quickly worried about coyotes or wild animals in the night air. I sat back down in the seat of my car but left the door open with the latch not around it all. Feeling comfortable about my surroundings at this. I light my joint and relaxed with my arm resting on the window frame. I started to notice a light flickering in my rearview mirror, which made me sit up at attention and turn my head all the way around. The little flickering light began to sway back and forth in a swaying motion, just like I would see across the mountain at my father's home previously. Mind you, there is not one soul in sight in the entire area. Just me and the smoke drifting out of my car. I realized I was alone with this light that grew brighter and brighter. Then it started glowing bigger into an orb. A gigantic ball of fire flew directly at me from 0 to 60. I grabbed my face and ducked my head in fear. I was screaming 'No". Then, as fast as it came towards me, it was nowhere in sight. A giant flash bang! I could not comprehend what I just experienced, but I knew it was not from this world. I closed the gate latch on my car and started my car. I peeled out of the dirt road area so fast that the rocks went flying like rain. I turned around in curiosity. I had to see where it was coming from.

There had to be a person or something down that way. I drove back down the road slowly with a keen eye on the environment, sky and surroundings. That's when I saw two vehicles parked diagonally from one another in the main lot by the restrooms. No headlights or taillights had pulled up or left in the little time I had been there. The two cars had each a man standing to the side of it. They were standing perfectly postured and in the same military style. I began to scream at them, "who are you? What was that? but got no response or body movement. It was as if they couldn't even hear me. I grew very uneasy about being so far out in the dark county mountain side with these men and got the heck out of dodge. I was very emotional and had my eyes filled with tears when I drove down the high-way. I was scared at that point to stay out in the dark country by myself after what I had just witnessed. I never shared this experience with anyone until I wrote this book. I believe that today, it was the Holy Spirit, and God showed Himself to me. Right in my face. He chose me to see Him, and he gave me the courage and the supernatural strength to defeat these devils that were hot on my heels to take my soul. It was so supernatural.

The next week, I stayed at the Howard Johnson in Ceres and put out an escorting ad. I had a few appointments that were coming and were ready when the first person knocked. I opened the door, and he said look, you have a lot of fans waiting out here. I stuck my head out but was not nervous about his statement. He then came into my room, and we did our thing. He then told me that he was from Bohemian Grove. I was not sure what that was, and I sent him on his way and went about my night. The next day, though, I got online and typed in Bohemian Grove. Wows, my eyes grew so big and swallowed deep. I even felt a little faint about what I was reading about the man I had just met. I had never heard of this group, not in any of my research. I was shocked that I had really been in the presence of a member of a true secret society. I learned that they are a political group as well as celebrity elites that get together for two weeks in the hills of Napa Valley, CA. These official men's club invite hookers, sex workers, prostitutes, and escorts. These women would be involved in a two-week party. At least have them lulled into a false reality. They are performing satanic rituals. They worship a giant owl statue called Molech, and they perform blood sacrifices, too. Molech is also known as Baal. In the bible, the pagans would worship Baal or Molech, who kill babies and sacrifice innocent human beings to their God. The God, is better known as the God of this world, the devil. This secret society is keeping these deprived traditions alive to this day. This modern-day area of society does not even realize that there are groups of people still performing these ancient rituals. Upon the innocent in the world right under the world's noses. I was almost a sacrifice. A Pawn Sacrifice. My God is omnipresent and sees all. He was never going to allow his faithful child to be taken out of the world by such evil wickedness. I know these cult members are aware of how real my God is today. No doubt!!! They can no longer deny The Lord's validity simply because I am still walking this earth and have breath in my lungs. With the rituals and graveyard spells, death magic and candle magic repeatedly done upon me, there is no other explanation then God! Since the beginning of time, they have been doing the same rituals throughout the centuries without any hiccups or failures. I had been seeing Mark from Atwater every weekend, but one Friday he said he was going to go to Lake Tahoe with his family. He invited me to come to see him there. He did not invite me to go with his family but to drive my car up and meet up with him. I thought it was kind of rude, but I still decided to take him up on his idea. I drove my car up and got a room. I called him, and his parents dropped him off to spend the night with me. We shared the night together, and I dropped him off with his family at their timeshare. When I got back to Modesto, I then went to use my bank card to rent a hotel room, but it wouldn't work. I was so confused as to why. I contacted the bank and then learned someone had changed my email to their email and changed my phone number to their number as well. I had no clue as to who could have done this to my bank account. They basically made my bank account their bank account. I was lucky to have spoken to a customer service representative that believed me when I told her I was the account owner, and this information was changed without my permission. Mark had taken my bank card information when he was with me in Tahoe and done this to me behind my back. It took me years to realize he was, in fact, doing harm to me while pretending, as he would say," build my empire."

I was also seeing a man named David quit often. I was not aware he was a member of The Bohemian Grove. He was sent in and paid by them from the beginning to love bomb me, too. I was completely blind, never thinking these men were perpetuating harm upon me. I only saw them for the masks they all wore. I only saw the good in these men. I never knew that such evil even existed in the world. I felt they were both sexy and sweet, but I always had the nonstop underlying feeling of betrayal always lingering in the background. I would always let them know that I felt something was off and that they should tell me what was really going on because they were going to get caught up. I felt it in the bottom of my soul. Dave eventually said, "Great, now they are being mean to me now because I was nice to you." I was so glad to get some kind of truth even though I didn't get the totality of "who" they were. Just another piece of the puzzle.

This puzzle piece was a big chunk of my story. I saw beneath the story and knew it was this group. I had pulled into a canal bank in Turlock for the night. I decided to watch Netflix. I chose a documentary called Bad Vegan about Sarma Megelanis. As I was watching this woman's story. I couldn't help but notice that her story was very similar to mine even though it was very different due to her lifestyle and the business that she had. I could see that the same people who were hurting me were most definitely the same ones that had hurt her. It was as if a light bulb went off in my mind. It was my ah ha moment for me. I finally had a true connection to another person's story in my real reality. It was the connect the dots in my research. It was July and very muggy that night. It was magical, as if the stars knew I was getting what they were telling me and guiding me to. My truth. Because all of a sudden, a huge thunder and lightning storm came together right over Atwater Ca which was about 30 min away from my location. I could see and hear it hitting the earth with its forcefulness and glorious light show. I felt as if God himself was telling me you're on the right track and made this a personal show of his power and wonderful miracles. The location of this storm was also a significant sign as well because this was the location of Marks's home in Atwater. I was in awe as to my Father's way of connecting with me. Bad Vegan had the elements of Hollywood, Alec Baldwin, Owen Wilson, secret societies, Black Opps operation, Blackwater, soul collection, mass amounts of money, thieves, traveling all over and disappearing for times. They had taken her for 400 million dollars, and she ended up with a ruined reputation and was put into prison. The one part of her story that made me realize her story and all these things were connected to my life was when her friend who was interviewed said MEAT SUITS. I was omg. That is what Jeannie had said. She had said they wear meat suits, and so did this lady. I felt the confirmation of the similarities. Intuitively, I began to understand that Hollywood was involved in the nightmare I was living in. I highly recommend you watch Bad Vegan yourself to understand what I am speaking about.

I knew this group wanted to work with me. They had someone contact me to make a porn movie, and I set up an appointment with one of their agents twice, but both times I did not go. I felt convicted by God for even thinking about doing such acts. If I was to choose to work with the sex industry, my soul would be contaminated and would be no longer a source for God. Fame and fortune were presented to me, but I was not interested in being famous for such things. I wanted to be famous for exposing these people. I used to tell them, "We can all be famous together". I knew what was happening to me was unheard of to the world. When they would laugh at me, I would tell them, "One day, I am going to have the last laugh, and they shall not inherit the earth. It has already been written". I would also stand out in the parking lots of the hotels and yell, "I don't want to be a part of your sex cult".

I knew I could have went and made a lot of money had I been involved with this group. But I knew they were demons, and once I saw them as so I could not unsee them. These were demons who thought they were going to trick me with their black magic and spells. I followed the directions of my Father God. He wouldn't lie to me, and I knew His promises would never fail me. He guarded me, He saved me, but He also gave me the free will to choose my path at that moment in time. Weeks went by and I was watching the movie Dirty Dancing. I have always had this thing with faces and could recognize people even years later or actors in movies when they were younger I had never seen. I felt this was a skill I had. As I was watching

Dirty Dancing, I noticed that the actress who played Penny, the lead dancer in the story, looked very similar to Sarma Melngailis from the Netflix documentary "Bad Vegan." I immediately looked up the name of the actress from Dirty Dancing. Her name is Cynthia Rhodes. I read all about her life, and it said she had died in a drug deal in New York. Sarma and Cynthia had the same smile, freckles, and mole. I went back online the next day, and I typed in Cynthia Rhodes, and a different actress popped up on the screen named Lee Ann Baker, who was a background dancer in Dirty Dancing. I was so confused because it was not Cynthia who I was intending to research. Lee Ann Bakers was in a movie called Necropolis. This a movie was about an evil witch reincarnated in modern day New York in the form of a beautiful Vespa riding punkette. To maintain her eternal youth status, she must sacrifice a virgin and find a sacred ring which holds tremendous power. I was guided to research the similarities in the looks of these women, which lead me to learn about necromancy. Doing more research and after watching this movie, I found necromancy in the bible. This is something the pagans were involved in biblical times and still participate in today. I was letting my curiosity lead me. I gained knowledge in an ancient practice that my enemies were using. Even though it was a movie and sounded so far out there, I knew I was led to research this topic because I needed to know my enemy. I felt I had a hand up on them after learning something they had no clue I was capable of knowing. Surprise to my enemies. I realized that spells and magic were, in fact something that was happening to me. Knowing and being aware was half the battle.

CHAPTER 7

I JUST KEPT GOING

One time, I had gotten a contact lens in my eye and could not get it out. I was in a panic and asked the front desk to call 911. I was told she would call for me. I waited like 30 min. My eye was watering immensely, causing complete blindness. I detected the phone buttons and called 911. When the operator answered the call, she stated," I am sorry you have the wrong number". I was quite sure if what she had said was really what she said. So, I called 911 again. When the call was answered, I told the 911 operator. "I needed an ambulance; I cannot drive because I have a contact stuck in my eye." The operator again said, "You called the wrong number"! I knew I hadn't called the wrong number. I was very confused and began to walk to the hospital, but I couldn't see anything. I was blinded, basically. I started to have a panic attack and was scared as to what was happening to me. This was the first time I was being gaslighted by the community besides the police officer that told me well it can't be everyone. I have called 911 a few times in my life and have never been told or heard of anyone being told you have called the wrong number. 911 is for everyone, I had thought.

I ended up down at the Walmart parking lot, trying to call anyone who would answer their phone for a ride to the hospital. But no one was answering me. I crawled in between some bushes, curled up into a ball and began to cry. I was scared and confused for the first time in my life. I began to call upon my warring angels for protection once again. The prayer warriors that taught me about God and what to do when evil was present is exactly what I did. I knew without fail that my angels would hear me. I finally gained my eyesight back and didn't know if the contact was still in my eye or not, but I was able to focus enough to walk back to the hotel. When I got back to the hotel, I packed my things and left. I was so upset and uneducated on gang stalking. I didn't understand my own life. In my frustration, as I walked by a canal, I threw my phone in the water. I felt like they couldn't watch me or keep track of me anymore. But I was wrong. They seemed to encamp everywhere I was, and I could feel them in the spirit and in the 3 D. These people would do things to me constantly that seemed so normal to the naked eye you wouldn't see it unless it was happening to you. Some stores would even reject me from shopping in their stores. They would lock the doors or simply just say I wasn't allowed in their store. One time, I was sitting at the gas station on Lander Avenue in Turlock, CA. Having my lunch. The way this gas station is set up is a circle formation. You can pull in one side and circle around to the other side to exit. I noticed vehicles circling me. The vehicles had old people, young people, couples, families, and single parents with their children staring and laughing at me. I can tell you it had to be at least 100 cars that day that swarmed me. Then, not only this was happening, but a military vehicle that was like a tall tanker of some sort pulled in as well. I instantly knew that they were trying to intimidate me with this display of power, but the funny thing is I was not scared; I was even more interested, and this gave me more things to investigate in my research as well. The military vehicle only validated the fact that I knew the Government was in on what was happening to me. I was still declaring out loud that you're going to get caught one of these days. I believed this with all my might. I just knew this would not go unpunished.

I knew I was not out of mind or crazy, and I needed to prove this to myself. I decided to drive down to L.A. just to see if the same things would be happening and if I would be followed. I left at nighttime, pulled over a few times and ended up pulling into an orchard right outside of Fresno. I had this car tarp that I would put over my car for privacy, so I got out and placed it on my car. As I was putting it on, I got a little nervous because it was so very dark and black outside. No moon or any light whatsoever. Not even a streetlight. I fell asleep for a few hours, peeked my eyes outside a hole in the tarp, and noticed a bright light around my car. I knew darn well that it was dark when I went to sleep and was not sure what was going on. I had to get out and see where this light was coming from. I emerged from my car, stepped my feet on the road, and just stood there in amazement. The entire sky and glow came from an unknown source; it was simply bright and light up, and I was no longer in the dark. This was the first time I had this happen to me. I automatically knew it was supernatural and welcomed it. Over the years, this has happened when I tried to park in the light. Every time. My Angels were putting the light on them. I lived it. I saw it with my own two eyes.

I proceeded on my research mission for truth, and nothing had changed. The one-headlight cars, the horns, the people laughing, holding their phones, standing in my personal space. I got the bright idea of driving to Malibu just to do my own experiment. I was only awakened more and more by the world beyond even though I was living in another at the same time. I went almost all the way to Vegas on another escapade of knowledge. I was going to see my ex, Bobby. I had almost gotten there and needed better directions, so I called him. I asked him for clearer directions, and he started playing stupid with me. This is a very smart man who I used to talk on the phone with for hours, but this time, he started playing dumb with me as If he didn't know the directions. I knew he was not acting right ,so I hung up the phone on him and ended up turning around. On my way back home, I got gas and didn't know how to get back on the freeway. So, I made an illegal move across the roadway to get to the entrance. I just got onto the freeway and noticed an unmarked vehicle behind me with lights going. I had never been pulled over by an undercover car in my life. The officer got out of the car and approached my window. He didn't even have an official uniform on. He was wearing street clothes and a bulletproof vest on. He asked me where I was going and asked for my license. I assumed he saw I was not from the area by my address and asked me what I was doing so far from home. I told him I came to see the ocean and take a vacation. Then he made a statement," Oh, we have been watching you for a long time". I was feeling uncomfortable with the way he said they had been following me for a long time now. He gave me back my license and sent me on my way. It was the weirdest incident I had ever had with a police officer.

Another problem that started for me was ordering from Amazon. I would order items, and my orders would not come or would be canceled. I mean, every time, my orders were messed with. It got to the point where I had to start asking other people to order things for me. I even used someone's account a few times with no issues, but then it began to happen again. It was as if they knew the orders were for me. This was an eye-opener for me. This cult just was letting me know they were controlling every aspect of my life.

CHAPTER 8
TARGETED NATION

I found an online group called Targeted Nation, Targeted Individuals, and a video by a young black man named Mayron May. His story touched my heart. Because what was happening to him was most definitely happening to me. He was an assistant district attorney and very well-spoken about how gang stalking and how it is done. He described it down to the T. I felt for him as I watched his videos. He even spoke about God and how he asked God to forgive him for what he was about to do. He affected me very profoundly with his words to his trauma, and I knew he wasn't crazy because what he was talking about was, in fact, happening to me. The day I found his video. I declared to him and vowed to get his good name back for him one of these days. I also found a story about Gavin Long, a young black man who was a military officer who was an active shooter on his base. He had a similar story and was labeled crazy, too. His story was the same. He was being followed, harassed, and all the aspects of gang stalking.

I came across another story involving Alex Alexis, who had the same gang stalking stories. But yet, he was also a young African American man. I have always been interested in the television channel Investigate I.D. This channel is about solving murders, cold cases, fresh cases. It's all about murder. The show The Evil Next Door I watched often. I happened to be watching this show one day and was appalled as to how this group of neighbors from this community in Pittsburgh was throwing his name in the mud. These neighbors were always pointing fingers at this one black man in their neighborhood, who they said was crazy and a troublemaker. As I listened to them talk badly about this black man who is now dead. I was shocked as I looked up this man's name, Everston Brown. His story led me to see that he had been in front of the white house with posters and billboards asking for help from the Government, stalking him through the MK Ultra program. I was blown away at what I was finding out about this man and angered by the individuals sitting on television disrespecting this man, who they all knew they had killed as a cult. At the end of his story, he is labeled a murderer, and they blow up his own home. I said to myself these people need to be exposed for the murders they are. How dare they sit on television and dismantle this man. An innocent man they had poked and poked at for years like vultures feeding off his pain. Knowing the true reality of what they were doing to him without any concern for him or anyone they had harmed for their sickness and discussing reasons for energy harvesting.

Looking online, I found an article about a wreck on Sunset Blvd. in Los Angeles CA. Where the police were involved, a man died. This is the story of Keenan Anderson, a third-grade teacher from Los Angeles California. He was perceived as crazy and resisting the police. The news only protected the gang stalking tactics that law enforcement uses upon innocent people all over the world. I watched the actual video of the incident on police video recordings and immediately recognized that, yet again, these were false situations. He was set up, and he was murdered by the L.A. Police. He was yelling on the video; they're going to kill me! And guess what they did. He was dead four hours after his arrest. I could see the fear in his eyes and felt all his confusion. He looked so lost and nervous as they were attacking him in daylight with everyone watching. It looks so normal, but it's not. Not if you know. You can't unknow what you know, and unsee what you have had to pleasure to see. It had been placed there forever and forever. Having been burned into my psyche left as a superpower to protect my mind. They were killing without touching people. Turning your own fears and confusion into an inner monster of turmoil and toil if unaware of these tactics. They perform these tactics day and night and night and day. It is designed to make you just be so overwhelmed to the point that you would give up on yourself. They would create such a massive amount of stress and confusion you would simply give up on yourself and your soul. They want you to commit suicide from all the trauma they cause on purpose. Shame on the devil. The devil needs to know you can't force people to love you. They were so very proud of themselves and thought their plan was such a great idea. Acting only on the demands of the devil. Plotting on how to destroy all my happiness. They tried this and that. They did it all ten thousand times over. How can you get enjoyment by creating harm to others? Finding the stories about the 5 African American men dealing with the same burdens brought me to realize something. The torture was not about our race. It seemed to be from the naked eye that all these things were meant to be racially driven. To keep the racial disconnect in our society up. To shape the narrative the direction of racism. Like gang stalking was about white power, hate of different races, or Klu Kluk Klan involvement, but I knew I had been arrested falsely multiple times; I had been abused and beaten by the police many times. One time my eye was blood red for 3 months. Bruises up and down my body, and when I contacted a lawyer about the incident ,I was told it was street justice. So, looking at my life as a white woman with freckles experiencing the same exact abuse and civil rights lawsuits. These cases have made me see that this gang stalking targeted individuals is not about race. It is about energy, the energy of our souls. Most definitely not about racism but about the internal souls each of us holds. We are in these physical vessels to live and follow our purpose on this earthly plain. The Bible says we do not fight flesh and blood, but we fight the principalities of darkness in the heavenly realm.

What was happening to me and others online was most definitely spiritual warfare. It's so real the devil disguises it under the premise of racism. With racism, he can cause strife and division amongst the people instead of allowing the world to see what the brutality is truly about. It's about our souls. The devil wants you to look over here while he's over there doing something behind the scenes. Just like a magician and his bag of tricks. Racism is not the problem it's the devil the using people as his vessels to hide in so he can keep his bloody war against humanity going to ensure he gets as many souls as he can before his time is up. This way, it goes unnoticed by the world. But I saw right through the lies with the Word of God. The word of God was taught to me in prison. I had to remember what I was taught to do in the presence of evil, I applied those directions from the bible, and they worked. I am not even a full knowledge holder of the Word of God. I thought I was full grown in the Word, but I see I am a toddler. After what I have been through. I am still refining my knowledge and growth. I am healing daily. I search to grow in my soul's path and my righteousness to glorify the Lord through my pain and my suffering. The more we suffer, the stronger he becomes. I am standing firm in the promises of my Father. He is the truth, the way and life forever. He will never forsake or leave me. I declare I am the proof that The Highest is real. God wants to save our souls, and the devil wants to destroy them and drag us to hell. Simply by using our weakness against us. I let God have my pain and worries. I let God fight my battles, vengeance will be the Lords. Do not touch my anointed ones. I feel I beat the devil at his own game with love, compassion, forgiveness and self-control.

After all the others I had found online in need of help, suffering in silence. I decided to make a day out of it and head to the main F.B.I. Head office in Sacramento, California. I packed my things and headed out. I made it into Sacramento and spent the night in my car, and that next sign of daybreak, I pulled into the F.B.I. I was a little nervous, but I knew I had to tell the truth. No matter how crazy my story sounded, I needed to help somehow and reach out to authorities. I approached the security office and went in. I spoke to the officers inside in charge and was told to wait for an investigator to come to come and speak to me. I waited inside a little interview room still located in the security office for about 20 min, but I never made it into the physical building F.B.I. building. An investigator came in the room and introduced himself. I asked him if he had ever heard of gang stalking? He replied that he had never heard of it. I began to see how this is a serious situation that really needs looking into. I explained to the agent how I did research and told him about these horrific atrocities that were happening to innocent people all over the world. It seemed as if he believed me but was a little off-set. I asked him for a business card in case I had more information for him but was met with yet another block in that matter. He said he didn't have business cards. The moment he stated that he didn't have cards, I felt as if I was being redirected to one of their fake people. I left the F.B.I. office and never spoke to anyone from their office ever again. I felt as if I did my part by reaching out to the proper authorities. I was always met with disregard by law enforcement, and this was very frustrating for me as you can imagine.

CHAPTER 9

JOHNNYS MURDER

I had mentioned my friend Johnny Morgan earlier in the book. This was a friend of mine who had always been there for me in my times of need. We had even ,packed together so that if I was not married by the time I was 45, we would marry one another, so we weren't alone. It was kind of a joke we had. I really did care for him as a friend deeply. I was not interested in being in a relationship with him. We had dated for a while in 2005, and I found him more of a friend. Our relationship was not based on sex. He treated me like a person and not a toy. When the gang stalking started, I went up to Johnnys house up in Mi-Wuk to stay with him a few times. I would sit in his front room, and I could see they had followed me to his house. Cars would pass all day and all night honking. The usual traffic in that area was not this heavy for the season. Especially at night. It was always dead, but not when I was there. He lived off Highway 120, heading up to dodge ridge ski lodge. I did not mention what was happening to me to Johnny because I did not want him to think I was crazy. I simply just pretended everything was ok. His dog Blazer, whom he had for many years, had just passed away. He was depressed over this. I was sad for him because he was his best friend. He did just get a new puppy to replace Blazer, so it alleviated some of the loss. I stayed with him for a few days and told him I would come back soon. I had gone down to Turlock and stayed with Christian. When I got to his house, he had been shot in the thigh very close to his penis. I asked him what happened, and he said he did it to him self by accident. I got the inclining he was lying because he was embarrassed. He got shot by someone. He did run with a rough crowd and was not the nicest person. He was sitting on his bed in his room and I went into his living room and noticed small holes in his ceiling. I investigated the holes, and I concluded that they were either bullet holes or holes for cameras to hide in his attic area. I felt he was spying on me, or this group had him put cameras in his house to catch me doing something wrong. I did not mention the holes to him and just kept it to myself. I did not want to alert him I was on to the fact that I knew he was working against me. If he knew I was checking things out at his house,. I wouldn't have been allowed to continue with my investigation. I stayed a few days and left. A few weeks later, I ended up back at Johnnys house. I went into Johnny's room and noticed he had moved his bedroom to the back bedroom. I asked him why. He said he just didn't want to be in that room anymore. I left it at that. I ended up staying in his old room that night and noticed the same holes I had seen at Christians's house in Johnny's ceiling. They were the exact same size and amount of them. I was freaked out a little bit. I felt this was related to this cult. I chose not to say anything about what I saw to Johnny to ensure no one knew I was on to them. I was feeling some kind of way about Johnny possibly being a part of it as well. I was sure I had a true friend in him and couldn't imagine him turning on me, too. That night, as I was lying on the bed and resting. Johnny was in his room asleep. I began to hear him yelling loudly. He was screaming 'get off me bitch, no, no, no, get off me bitch" over and over again. He did this for about 20 minutes, when I had the thought that maybe he's going to try to get me in trouble and say I was doing something to him if the neighbors were to call the police. He was yelling so loud that I turned on my video camera and began to record what was going on in order to cover my butt. He continued to scream and yell for about an hour. I thought he was being attacked by a demon of some sort because I got up to make sure no one was in his room with him but saw no one there. I asked him if he was ok, but he wouldn't respond. The next morning, he acted like he did not know what I was talking about when I inquired about the incident. We had a friend named Eian who stopped by for breakfast. Johnny and I wanted to eat on the porch, so we all went outside. The weather was nice,, and the sun was shining. Across the street, a man pulled in the driveway and parked. He stepped out of his vehicle with a bunch of balloons and just stood there looking at us with a creepy smile on his face. He was just staring, and he reminded me of the clown in the movie IT. I saw that Johnny was getting nervous, and he told me not to look at him. He was standing like that for about 10 minutes when I stood up and said, "what's your problem"? When I did that, Johnny begged me to stop and ignore him. He seemed scared of this man, which was not normal to be a scaredy cat, He was very manly and always stood up for himself. So, for me to see him acting timid and backing down to someone I knew, this man had done something to Johnny. When Johnny went inside the house, Eian told me a few days before, the man was videoing Johnny and bullying him. Eian saw it all. I did not mention what Eian had told me to him but filed it in my mind in case something happened to Johnny.

I did not see him for a while but the next time I showed up, he wouldn't open his door for me and told me to leave. It was strange behavior for him. He opened his door just enough so I could see his eyeballs peek out. He was rude to me and told me to leave. I was hurt and shattered and thought to myself oh no, they got to Johnny. He did that to me a few more times. I continued to stop by his house to check on him often, even though he wouldn't let me in. It was a trip to head up the hill that far, but I was worried about him. He wasn't acting right. He lived in a duplex with new neighbors that had just moved in next door, whom I had never met. I knocked on his door, but there was no answer. I thought he was there because his puppy was on the dog leash in the backyard, and it was cold and snowing outside. I knew that he wouldn't leave his animal outside like that and then leave. He was a good pet owner and was never negative. He never left the hill in all the 14 years I knew him. He hated leaving his house. I went around to the backyard and noticed his bathroom window was cracked just slightly. I decided I was going in. I slid the window open and climbed in. I opened the front door and went out to get the puppy.

I looked around the house and called out for Johnny in case he was hiding from me. I realized he was really gone and grew concerned for him. I started to clean up his house so when he showed back up, he would be happy to see his home clean. I was there all day waiting. When I was cleaning, I came across some notes he had written, and one certainly caught my attention. It said" nothing's changed since the change". It made me think of how he was yelling that night I stayed. The way he was acting that night was as if he was being possessed. Nothing has changed since the change. What change, a demon that entered him, was my feelings. I folded the note and put it in my pocket. Then I found another note that said, 'My landlord has been calling my sister and threatening her". I put that note in my pocket, too. My intuition was telling me something was wrong. I grew very stressed when the sun had gone down, and Johnny did not come back. His car was even in the driveway, which made this situation odder. Where was my friend? I went next door and asked the neighbors if they'd seen johnny or knew where he was. They said no and said they did not like Johnny. I then walked to the house next door and asked them if they knew. I did not know these people either, but they seemed to know Johnny well. They had said Johnny was in jail. When he got arrested, he gave them his bank card. Johnnys' father had left him a trust fund many years ago, and that is what he lived on, and he knew he wouldn't just hand over his money to these strangers. I walked back to Johnnys duplex and chilled inside with his puppy. As I was sitting in the living room, I heard a loud knock on the door and heard the neighbors telling me I needed to leave, and I couldn't be in Johnnys house and they were going to call the police. This was my friend's house, and I couldn't understand why these strangers were varying so much about me being in his house. It was none of their business. I told them I wasn't leaving and to mind their business. About 45 minutes later, there was another knock with the announcement that it was the police. I snatched up the puppy and ran into Johnny's bedroom. The police knocked and knocked, and then they opened the door, and I heard them yell my name. I freaked out because how did they know my name? I held the puppy and sat very still on the bed. I didn't make a sound, but they continued to just yell my name and tell me I needed to come outside. I know the law and know the police could not come inside without a warrant. Eventually, they left. I was tripping out because the police had come for me when I was not doing anything but wait for my friend to come home. I stayed for 3 days, and he never came home. The neighbors were very rude and made me uncomfortable. I was so worried about him but I ended up leaving and leaving the puppy there in the house with food in a bowl. I didn't want to take the dog because I knew that would make him mad. I had contacted the jail and asked if Johnny was an inmate, and they stated that he was not in jail. I knew right there something was wrong. The neighbors had said he was there and had his bank card. They straight lied to me. I also looked up his name and found he was placed on the terrorist watch list and noticed I was on this list as well. I was really concerned about his safety and what had happened to my friend. For weeks, I called his phone repeatedly. With no answer, it went straight to voice mail every time. I was so happy when I eventually did receive a text message back from him. I couldn't get him to call me, though. I felt satisfied with knowing he was home and he was ok with the text messages I had received. About two weeks had gone by, and I thought I would randomly show up at his house without calling. I drove by his house slowly and noticed a strange car in the driveway. I did not see Johnny, but I saw a lady sitting on his porch. I did not know if this was his girlfriend or something and just drove away. I did not want to cause him problems in any way, especially in his love life. Months went by, and I was at the car wash in Twain Harte washing my car. I had run into a mutual friend of mine and Johnny's while there. We were chopping it up for a while when he mentioned hey, did you hear Johnny died? I couldn't believe what he had said. I broke down and started crying and was shocked as to how he died. My friend said Johnny hung himself. I told him I had driven by and saw a strange car with a lady I didn't recognize at his house around the time he said it happened. He replied that it was probably his sister cleaning out his house. I needed to do some investigating into this news. I drove straight to the neighbor's house, which had his bank card, thinking they were spending his money. I asked them the story of what had happened, and I was told Johnny had been hanging around some tall guy recently he had just met. That guy had found Johnny hung with a sheet in his room when he came over to visit him. The strange guy then notified the police that Johnny was dead, and they came and closed the case as a suicide. The police also let this stranger drive off in Johnny's car. I was so angry with what I heard. The police just let this man take his car and did not investigate the incident as a crime or murder at all. For all the truth could have been, this strange guy had murdered Johnny. My feelings about his death are he did not kill himself. He was taken out by this cult because I had done my research about these people, and if certain people don't get on the bad wagon of the hate train against the targeted individual, they will just kill you. I know this cult killed my friend because he did not want to hurt me. He was my one true friend, and they killed him. I don't even really know if Johnny was the one that texted me those messages. It could have very well been one of them pretending to be him.

CHAPTER 10

THE GREAT SET UP/POLICE HARASSMENT

I had a car accident and flipped my car three times. I passed a car on a double yellow line, and I took full responsibility for the wreck. It had been snowing in Sonora weeks prior, and they had put a lot of sand on the road to keep people from sliding in the snow. But after the snow had melted, the sand went into the middle of the road. So, when I went around the car, my tires hit the sand, which caused me to tailspin. I was swaying back and forth and then started to do a 1/80. Then, my car slammed right into the back of a car in front of me. When I hit the car, my car slipped over and then again. I landed upside down. The funny thing is God told me to strap my seat belt across to the passenger buckle, which made me super tight in the seat belt. I listened to what God had said, and I believe that God knew I was going to wreck. He saved my life. He has saved me so many times. I had hit another vehicle and was concerned about the car I hit, but the car was pushed off a cliff side. I was freaked out that I had hurt someone badly. I got out of my car and ran to the cliff side. I looked down and saw someone standing straight up outside his driver's side window. I ran down to see if he needed help, and that's when the ambulance showed up, but my car was totaled. I no longer had a car and had nowhere to live or stay at all.

I was waiting for my insurance money from the accident to come in to purchase another car. I was still escorting but only minimally with certain people. I was too aware of the fake people smiling in my face but didn't know what it was about. I finally got my check for a new car and went and rented a car for a few weeks to find a new car to purchase. I decided to drive up to Miwuk Village, where my home was with my husband Daniel. I drove to my house where I had lived in with him. I had not seen him or spoken to him since I went to prison. I couldn't believe what I saw when I drove by. My beautiful little doll house home that I had just remodeled when all this went down looked like a bomb had gone off. Every window had boards nailed to them, and the pain job was messed up with graffiti on it the front door windows were replaced with cardboard. The front yard was destroyed, with garbage spread all over the place, and cars were wrecked in the driveway. I was shocked to see what I saw. I pulled into the driveway and parked my car. I could tell that no one was living there, so I walked to the back door and went into the house. I tried the electricity, and it was on. I walked through my old home with disdain on my face. I couldn't understand why the house was abandoned and left in such disarray. I decided to stay and clean up the house and the yard. I had nowhere to stay at the time, and it was so far away in the mountains that I felt the stalking wouldn't be as easy for them to do, but I was wrong.

The stalking still was happening because the first morning at my old house. I woke up to an entire crew of tree trimmers in the backyard with chainsaws running loudly and getting started on the trees. I ran out and shut down the whole project and asked them to leave the yard. I was not surprised at what was happening because wherever I went or parked my car, the chainsaws, mowers, and leaf blowers were always blasting in full force. 24/7. None stop. I don't know why I thought it would not happen up in the mountains. They only followed me. I had stayed there a few weeks, but one morning, I was putting on my make-up when I heard the front door bust open. I was not sure that I heard what I heard, but I went into the living room and saw the front door open. And I heard the police yelling my name and directing me to come outside. I walked over to the door and poked my head out. That is when the officers grabbed me by my arms ,turned me around and threw handcuffs on me. I was then placed in the back of a cop car. I was telling the cops that it was my home with my husband. They were going to arrest me. But then they opened the door and said just for me to get my things and leave the house. I wouldn't be arrested if I just left the house. I went back into the house and started packing my things up to get out of there. As I was packing my car up, the police officers apologized to me for what they had done. I understood why and accepted their apology. I loaded the car up and got on my way. I ended up finding a car lot in Merced that day ,found a car to lease and returned the rental car.

I was staying in my car and used to park my car in different spots to observe the world around me. I felt this would lead me to figure out what was happening to me. Observation was my new job in life. One day, I parked at a major gas station between Merced and Delhi off Highway 99. I was there for a few hours and videoing people and cars. A van had pulled right in front of my car, I videoed, but they were blocking my view some pulled out to the back of the building right by the entrance to the highway. As I was sitting there watching the car enter the highway, I noticed every car that was getting on the freeway had a person in the car that would touch their nose. I mean every car for hours and hours. I was kind of freaking out. But then I realized how much bigger this situation was than me. I finally saw the truth. God opened my eyes to see the reality of this magical world that had been hidden from me. I was telling myself I would not have bought my car knowing how much larger of scale this truly was. I was kicking myself in the butt. I knew I knew what I saw was real, and I was not having a delusion. I saw at least 100 or more cars with a person driving would touch their nose every time with out a break in between vehicles. I was meant to see this sight that day. I took in this information that God was showing me, but I never told anyone what I had discovered.

I had gotten 9,000 dollars for my wreck and spent about 6,000 at the car lot. Insurance and all. So, as you can imagine, I didn't have a lot left over to spend, but I have always been a frugal person. I ended up one night hanging out with a guy I met randomly. I spent the night at his house, and he offered me a pipe to take. I never liked to buy pipes or even have them. I don't know why I took it, but I did. I placed it deep into my laundry basket with dirty clothes in the back seat of my car. I ended up in Oakdale, California, at the gas station and went in to use the restroom. When I came out of the restroom, I noticed a police officer standing right next to my vehicle and leaning up on it with his arm. I didn't quite get it because I had done nothing wrong. When I walked up and approached the officer, he stated I needed to give him my I.D. I had gone to school for criminal justice, and I knew the law, so I didn't have to give him my license without probable cause. I asked the officer what it was I had done, and he said I ran a red light. I had not run a red light and was wondering why he didn't pull me over when I parked my car. He was nowhere around when I got out of the car. I started to tell the officer I was not going to be giving him my license when, out of the blue, another officer came from behind me and slammed me up against the car. And began yelling and quit resisting arrest. I was being set up. I knew it. I was beaten up, then handcuffed and tossed into the back of the cop car. That's when the police began searching for my car. I was at their mercy.

I had done nothing wrong and had no warrants. The search was not legal, and I knew it. I heard the office state that he had found the pipe and then told an older lady across the parking lot that he had found it and held it up. I knew the guy had dirty me up the night before because how did they know I had that pipe? There's no way. They arrested me and towed my car for no reason. I asked on the way to jail what the arrest was for and was given the simple answer I should have just given him my license. I was booked and released with a paraphernalia charge, but my car had now been towed. I had to find a ride to the tow yard the next day because the fees were stacking up, and they are not cheap at a tow yard. I had arrived around 11:45 a.m., and the woman stated she was going to go to lunch she would be back and instructed me to go get the police release first to get the car. I went to the police station and paid the 100.00-dollar fee for the release. I walked back to the tow yard, expecting the woman to be back to release my car. But no, she never showed up, and as I was waiting outside the locked building, the officer who arrested me began to harass me again. I then walked back over to the police station and demanded that I talk to the watch commander on duty. I was allowed to speak with him and a few of the other officers, along with the one I was complaining about. I got nowhere, and nothing was done to the officer. The justice system was becoming more and more of a joke to me at this point. I was still waiting to go to trial for my son hitting me in between all of this. I had even picked out the attorney I wanted to help me with the case, but my family made me take another one. One I didn't approve of was the simple fact of when I walked into his office, he had a picture of a wizard on his office wall. I knew he was not a man of God and didn't approve of him, but I was forced by my father to have him represent me. He never would contact me, either only my grandmother or my father. Which is against the attorney-client privilege, but no one seems to care about that either.

I only had 750.00 more to get my car payment to 129.00 a month to pay off the little spark I had bought. I went into the car lot to pay off this amount. I was told that the bank I had originally gone with had rejected me. I was now with another bank who required more money for financing. I gave them what I had and agreed to pay the rest later. I had gone to Tracy to work and didn't want to place an ad, because I needed to pay for my car. I placed an escorting ad, but I didn't get one phone call. I knew something was off, and now I was kicking myself for buying the car. I knew they were blocking my phone to so that I would not have clients and not make money. These people follow my every step and wanted to ensure that I wouldn't be able to pay for my car. I felt it with my intuition once again. God was letting me know that this was being done to me. I thought back to the people who were touching their noses at the highway entrance that day. I felt like, omg, there are so many of them and just one of me. Today, that's the angel army. They were on my side. The car I got was a joke. It started to have problems, and they wouldn't fix it even though I had taken it to their shop many times. I felt as if I was paying for a car that was not reliable at all. I had a few days left to make the money for my payment, but I just couldn't even want to escort or give them the satisfaction. I knew this even though it meant I could lose my car. I was not going to play this game with these invisible jerks who thought it was funny to control my life. I knew if I just didn't give them anything to control, it would take away their power. Even if that meant I was losing out. I was staying at Travel Lodge Lodge Hotel because the owner was giving me discounts on my stay. It was not the best place to stay, but beggars can't be choosers. I had my car parked in front of my room. When I heard the tow truck out front. I just knew it was for my car. Sure things. I ran outside, and the door shut behind me. I had my 200.00-dollar cowboy boots, the last of the pictures of my kids, paperwork, and clothes in the car. I asked the tow truck driver if I could get my things, but I didn't have the keys to get into the car, and they didn't either. I ran down to the hotel office and asked for a new key to my room. The guy at the desk was very aggressive and not wanting to give me a key, even though they had taken a copy of my I.D. I was running back to my car, and by the time I got there, they had loaded up my car on their truck, and it was heading out of the parking lot. I lost all my things in the car, including my car.

I had my trial coming up with my son for terrorist threats in Tuolumne County. It was October 2022, and I had asked my grandmother if I could stay with her for my trial because I did not have a car anymore to go back and forth from the valley back to Sonora. She let me come stay with her for a few days because my uncle Byron was living there at that time. When we pulled into the driveway, I saw my uncle had bought a brand-new pickup truck and was put off by the extravagant purchase. I just assumed he was living good on his retirement and was happy for him. I did not ask any questions. I felt it was none of my business. I knew he was totally addicted to oxycontin and spent over 4,000 a month on these pills. Around the same time, I had learned that my best friend Melisa had opened a business as well. I felt certain friends and family members of mine were never able to have such purchases or businesses in their lives before. My grandmother even asked me how did Melisa opened a business? I had no answer for her. I didn't get it or understand it myself.

She had told me to clean out the closet in her art room while I was there. I started to clean out the closet when I came across a Play Girl magazine. This was the weirdest thing I could have found at first of. Just by the few characters in the home to choose from. My grandmother was in her 80s, and I had snooped through her things my whole life, never having found anything perverted before. I knew it had to be Uncle Byron or Frank grandmas third husband's dirty little secret magazine. Play Girl is a naked man not a woman. So, someone in the house was gay. I just kept it to myself and did not say a word. I took the magazine and put it in my bag. I thought the men looked sexy, too. And it had a centerfold poster I thought I would use on my wall somewhere. I also came across a plastic bag of art that Franks's deceased wife had drawn. I love art,, and she is very talented, so I began to take each one out one by one and was very impressed by her talent. Each one I pulled out, I would stack it on the last one. I was making an order. I came across one paper that was not art. I began to read it. I was reading some kind of oath that Frank Had signed with the Navy. This paper had a statement and an oath stating that everyone will be respectful to Franklin Martin in this realm, the realm of mermaid sea serpents', crabs, dolphins, whales, fairies, Atlantis, and all kinds of mystical creatures. It also said he was a warlock. I was like, wow, Frank thinks he's Harry Potter! This was a cult called the Purple Dragons. Signed longitude and latitude. I did some research on them, and yes, there was a secret group of warlocks in the military. But I didn't say a word to my grandmother or anyone. I took this vow evidence and put it with my things for proof of Franks's weird secret life.

I then asked for a ride to town and had her drop me off at a hotel in Sonora. So I could be in town for my trial. In my hotel room that night, I pulled out that magazine, taped the centerfold picture of the hottie, and taped it to the bathroom door in the hotel. I called him boyfriend for the night. Lol. The funny thing is I forgot my phone in my hotel room. Frank and my grandma had come to supposedly support me at the courthouse for my trial. I asked Frank and Grandma to go get my phone from my hotel room and I gave them my key. I totally forgot that I had put that picture up on the bathroom door. That evening after the court was over, I was dropped off by Marylin and Frank. As I came in my room expecting to see Mr. Sexy looking back at me. To my surprise, Frank had ripped the poster off the bathroom wall. I knew it was not the maid at the hotel, because I didn't request maid service, and the bed was not made. I laughed to myself and realized that, wow,, that must have been Frank's magazine. So, in this little investigative search while grandma's was found to find two ways out realities. I found a wizard's oath and the Hot Boy magazine that really sealed the deal for me on him. I went through my 3-day trial and won the trial. I beat 5 felony charges by jury trial, which was very nerve racking. It was 3 days long, and justice was served. The most awful part of the trial was when my own son was even given immunity for stealing my things to get on the stand and told bold faced lies about me. Plus, Tuolumne County stated I had two strikes and wanted to give me three strike me. But justice was served on my behalf, and I won the court case. I only received resisting arrest and community service.

I had nowhere to go and ended up going back to my father's home right after winning this case. I had a restraining order to not be around Hannah and Hannah agreed to not have any problems. The very next week, my father was starting to a fight, knowing I had that restraining order saying I owed him for electric bill which I had been paying. He was simply starting a fight with me, and I didn't want to fight. He then said he was going to call the police on me. I was so upset that he was stating he would try to get me in trouble again. I pushed my way past him, and he did call the police. The police came and knocked on my door, but I had it locked and didn't answer. They left with no incident. I had thought it was over, but they ended up picking up more charges upon me, which I have yet to deal with. I am done dealing with these false cases. It's ridiculous that these police officers are connected to my family at the snap of a finger. It is nonstop and continues to happen to me to this day. I did move out of the house and have not been back since.

I still had one person I had kept in my inner circle, Mark. Mark had come to see me at the Travel Lodge in Turlock Ca., and I had asked him to take me to Taco Bell. As we were getting in his car, a woman came out of one the rooms in front of his car, and as she came out, they made eye contact directly and saw them both smirks at each other. I called it out and he said I was being stupid and that it didn't happen, but I knew I saw what I saw. Plus, my intuition had told me that they knew each other. It was June of 2022, and the fair had come to town in Turlock. Mark invited me to go with him to the fair, which made me happy because I had not been invited to go anywhere in such a long time that the idea was exciting to me even though he was not being honest with me. I took the bus over to the 99-cent store in Turlock just to get some false eyelashes for cheap. That was all I needed to get, but I got off track with impulse buys and began to shop. I hated to go shopping due to the weirdo that would harass me when I would go out. I put my headphones on to listen to a comedian on Netflix on my laptop as I was shopping, I simply to block out these people.

I was enjoying myself and not bothering anyone when, all of a sudden, one of the employees stopped me and stated I had bumped into another customer and that if it happened again, I will be asked to leave. I didn't know what she was talking about and said I do apologize for anything I had done. I continued to go along and shop and do me. I was looking at the chips and noticed them out of the corner of my eye. I noticed another lady from the store who was heading right in my direction. I knew she was coming to harass me. I then stopped her in her tracks and put my hand out with a stop motion. I pulled out my earphones and told her, "I don't even want to hear what you're going to say, I feel harassed, and I am calling the police". I grabbed my cell phone and called 911, but because my phone would not work. The woman was standing just staring at me. But I noticed she had the store phone and asked her to call the police. I then flipped my hair and said let's go wait by the front door for the police. She followed right behind me. As we were standing in the doorway of the store waiting, the employee punched me right in my nose. I grabbed my nose in utter dismay and stated out loud," This lady just punched me". I was expecting everyone around me to be concerned, but that was not the case. At that moment all the people in the store said in unison "No she didn't"! I was now really experiencing a lot of confusion I had never felt before in my life.

I immediately knew I needed to get out of this store. I pushed the cart to the side and headed outside the store doors. As I walked through the doors,, I saw a strange old man coming into the store who stuck his leg out to trip me, which he did. Then he proceeded to flip me the bird. I looked at him after he I caught myself from falling with eyes of disgust. Then, I threw my hands up in the air as if I did not understanding what was happening and asked that strange man what the heck are you doing? That's when I called 911 again and asked the police to come to the scene. I also turned on my computer to record and to protect myself from any more weird things I couldn't prove were happening. I walked down the sidewalk to the end of the shopping center. As I was walking down the sidewalk, I was recording the cars driving by me because the people in the cars were yelling at me and flipping me off. I was blown away by what I was witnessing. I felt as if I was in the twilight zone.

I waited for the police, and they showed up in about 5 minutes. I was told I was being held until the investigation was over. 2 hours passed when a sergeant pulled up and got out of his car. I asked him if he had seen the video, and he replied, "yes"! I said, "good" are you going to arrest her"? He said, "No, I am arresting you! , turn around." I couldn't believe what was happening to me because I had done nothing wrong yet again. I was arrested for attempted robbery and assault. I was facing 25 to life again with a bail of 250,000, and I was told I had two strikes again. I took the plea deal in 2015 when I went to prison. I only took the deal because it involved no strikes. The deal was I could go to rehab or prison for 9 years and 8 months, never thinking I would go to prison because I had never been to rehab. The judge gave me the 9 years and 8 months. I guess you can say I went hardcore rehab, which was straight to prison, no if ands or butts. I also was placed on parole for 3 years and was released early. I completed all the requirements needed to be released early, which rarely happens, my parole officer had told me. I completed all the requirements most people never even started. I never had a dirty drug test. I made every domestic violence class and paid all fees for the classes. I was never informed of any strikes by my parole officer. I even contacted C.D.C.R and got my sentencing paperwork sent to me, which stated I had no strikes. In between all the stalking, harassing, and thievery being committed against me, I had that paperwork stolen from me, just like everything else I had in my life, including my patient information, social security information, birth certificates etc.

I went to jail and was put into covid down-lockdown for 14 days in one cell with one woman. While in this cell with her, she made statements that I was one of the last of the naturals. I had no clue what she meant, but I put this information into my bank of files for my research into my life. I was locked in this room with this woman who had very bad gastrointestinal problems,' and she would release these pungent smelling flatulent that would stink up the entire room all day. I felt like I was going to pass out from this smell sometimes. Finally, they came and released us into the general population, and I was so relieved to get away from this woman. I went to my arraignment in video court, and that's when my bail was raised to 250,000. I then went to actual court for my pretrial. When I spoke with my public defender, he began to read off my charges and stated I was looking at 3 strikes case. When he said this statement, I wanted to stick up for myself, so I said, "Sir, I don't have any strikes." that's when he came back with," that's it, you're going to a mental evaluation'. I had already gone through the false strikes situation with Tuolumne County and couldn't understand how this was happening to me once again. I had been arrested a few times in my life and have never been told to go for mental evaluation. I was absolutely shocked by the injustice I was facing on top of the injustice I was already in. I went back to the jail, and a few days later, I was called out to meet with a psychologist for an evaluation. The woman who came to give me the evaluation and she was very kind. She only asked me a lot of political questions. These questions had nothing to do with my mental state of mind. She did not ask me anything about my mind or my thoughts. I thought this was odd. I was so glad that I had been keeping up with politics. I only started keeping up with politics because of what was happening to me. In previous years, I totally thought that the government had things under control,. I was then taken to a part of the jail called REACT. This was a dorm environment, with 8 women in each room. As you can imagine, this room was noisy and uncomfortable. I kept to myself while in this room because I got a bad vibe from the girls in it. One lady had called my breast prune tits when she had never seen my breasts. Then, we didn't get to go to recreation for 2 days, and we all decided to write a grievance against the facility. We had put my name on the top of the form, which meant the sergeant would be coming to talk to me about it. He came into the room to discuss the grievance and approached us, but when we were all asked about it, no one had my back, and they turned their backs on me. I was then pulled out of the room and placed at a table in the middle of the day room. This sergeant began to braid me in front of the entire unit of women. He then said this is what happens when you write a grievance. A bunch of other officers then came in and began to go through each unit and search for everybody's things. All the contraband was taken and thrown away on account of me. While they were searching for the units, we were all placed outside in the yard. So, I was thrown outside with 40 or so another woman who were not happy with me. I suppose this was to make me feel scared or intimidated somehow. I simply stood up to all these women who were talking crap to me. I told them all I knew what's right and what's wrong and that they were all spineless cowards. I stood my ground as to this fact. When we were placed back in the room, I pushed the button and asked to be moved. The officers came upstairs slammed me up against the wall, and put handcuffs on me. I then marched out of the unit as if I had done something wrong. I got a lecture from the sergeant about how I was putting their facility under chaos and causing a riot. Which was putting inmates' and officers' safety in danger. I was then moved to another unit, but I recognized someone I had gone to school with, and that made me feel at ease. This room ended up being a better fit for me. I was allowed to use the phone and first contacted my father, which was fruitless because he said he had no money to help me. I got hold of my grandma and explained to her I would pay her back out of the million-dollar sexual harassment case I was waiting on. To get bailed out. That evening,, Alladin Bail Bonds told me someone was going to pick me up. I was released and went outside to wait for my ride. I looked across the parking lot and thought I saw my best friend Melisa in the car I didn't recognize. She was driving a brand-new car, and I could not understand why she was even there in the first place. I had not spoken to her in months and didn't plan on speaking to her again. I hesitated to get in her car but decided to go with her because I knew she would start yelling and throwing a fit in front of the jail. I couldn't take that chance. I literally had just walked out of the jail and didn't want to draw any more attention to me. I went to her house for the night and had her take me to Sonora the next morning. I had her drop me off at Walmart. Before she departed from me, I wanted to let her know how I felt. I told her I knew she only picked me up and helped me because she thought I had my settlement money, and that was out. I didn't appreciate being used and didn't need a friend who was never there for me. Her jaw hit the floor, and she denied everything I was saying. Of course, but I didn't let the way I felt be pushed aside again. I knew she only came to get me because my lawyer for my sexual harassment suit had told my grandmother my settlement was settled and my money was coming in. Which is the only reason my grandmother bailed me out. I don't know why my lawyer told her that, but it was not true. Both vultures were just after money, and I knew it.

When I went to sign the paperwork for my bail, I was told about a man named Russell Blanter who had contacted them about my bail. I requested to have him removed from my paperwork, but they didn't really want to remove him. I didn't like that this stranger was all up in my personal business. I knew I had a huge mountain to climb, and I needed real legal help. I didn't want to go with Charles Smith again because of my gut feeling about him. My grandmother guided me to a lawyer named Gradford. He represented my father in his marijuana case years prior. I trusted that my grandmother was leading me to someone who would help me. She made an appointment to go talk to him about my case. Frank and my grandmother took me to the appointment and paid him 15,000 for him to represent me in my case. I believed that he was a good fit for my case, too. I went to tell him about my case a few times, and he showed me the video of the incident, and it was clear that I was set up, and he even stated it. He said that he had other clients that this had happened to in the past. This was nothing new to him. I was so happy that the video showed her hitting me and making a statement to the police officer when he asked if I was stealing, and she said, "no, she was just an uncooperative customer." My question was, exactly what an uncooperative customer is. All the other customers saying "no she didn't "was the best proof of what had happened to me. I am going to circle back around to this false arrest along with all the others in the near end, and it will all make sense to them, but first, let me share with you all more b.s. from the police directed by the freemasons towards me.

I ended up staying at Christians's house for a few days and put an ad out, hoping to make some money. I was texting this one particular man that said he wanted a sex slave. Now, when I think of this statement, I think of a fantasy, not really thinking that men out there really want a slave. If I would have known what I know now, I would never have answered this message. As I was texting him, one of Christians's girlfriends showed up and started a fight with me. She stated I had to leave. Then she threw a drink on my computer and hit me repeatedly. I didn't fight her back and just started laughing at her. I was telling her I was not going to fight you. I am out on 250,000 dollars bail, and you are not worth it. I had the men I was talking to come pick me up from Christians. This man was named Mike, and we became close friends, not just a client. He had a lady he was seeing in a different towna, and he let me stay in his beautiful home so I could work and have clients come over. This was perfect for me because I didn't have to pay for hotel rooms and deal with all the stalking and such by the cult. At least, that's what I thought at the beginning. This part of the story is when I first started to realize that someone was copying me and taking all of my clients. I had one client that would come at least once a month from Livermore Ca to see me, and he was always on time and never negotiated my price with me. I had made an appointment to see him and expected him at 6 P.M. that evening. When 6 rolled around and he did not show, I called him, only for him to state he had just left and he had seen me. I was confused by his statement. I knew I had not seen him and replied," what are you talking about you didn't see me. I was waiting for you. It's 6:15 right now. He said, 'I know, I got there early and saw you." I just hung up the phone and never called or answered his calls again. So now someone else had said I robbed them with a black man. Mark was using my profile to send other girls on my name, and now this client is saying he saw me when I know I did not see him. I was becoming aware that something very fishy was going on.

Mike was letting me stay at his home more and more, and we would openly talk about what was happening to me, but only in pieces. Things started happening at Mikes's house that were ultimate supernatural experiences that I had ever come across. One example was when we were sitting on his couch one night talking, and something hit the wall right behind his couch so loud and hard it made me jump, and I began to cry. He simply acted as if nothing happened. I had only experienced them at the hotels banging on the walls. I had never experienced it at anyone's home. He was also using the vacuum a lot and started up his loud machinery in his garage all the time, which was part of the noise harassment. This is what they do all the time. I could not go anywhere without a leaf blower, a lawn mower, a generator and such. Just loud noise harassment. Which I know today is what they do to block out the Holy Spirit's connections with you. If things are loud and distracting, you can't hear God. At least, that's what they thought. I was always talking to God about what was happening to me. I was always putting on my Amour of God daily. I would put on my helmet of salvation, my belt of truth, my breastplate of righteousness, and my shield of faith. I would draw up the sword of the spirit and, most importantly, my shoes of peace. In fact, I had a pair of vans shoes and painted them and made them my shoes of peace and wore them out til I couldn't wear them anymore.

The year was December 29, 2022, and Mike left one weekend and. I had a few clients coming and had one set for 4 A.M. I was waiting for him anxiously because I didn't want to fall asleep and miss our appointment. So, I kept going to the front door, standing on my tip toes looking through the peep hole. I turned the porch light on and off. I had been looking out of it for about 20 seconds when a supernatural force thwacked the door with all its energy. It was as if a giant man had ran from the street like a line-backer and slammed into the front door. Mind you, this door was a solid wood double door that was very sturdy. I was astonished by this experience, but I was not scared. The date I had been waiting for never showed up, and I went to bed without losing any sleep. I woke up the next morning thinking about the odd happening I had gone through, but I let it go and went about my morning. I then got in the shower and opened the drawer to block it from being opened, as well as locked the doorknob.

I took my nice, hot, steamy shower and was feeling clean and fresh. I opened the slider of the shower door, and blam… I looked out and then saw the bathroom door wide open. I stared down the hallway in blank amazement. I was not terrified in any way. I simply said out loud, "very funny, you don't scare me. If you're still here, reveal yourself"! but no answer or anything appeared. That night,, I went online looking for ghost movies or anything that had to do with entities that were invisible. I believe the Most High drew me to a movie called Entity from 1982. This was a story about Carla Moran, who was played by [Barbara Hershey], is raped and attacked by an invisible force. She begins therapy with Dr. Schneiderman, played by [Ron Silverman], a psychiatrist who believes Carla's traumatic past is motivating her to commit self-induced injuries rather than anything supernatural. When the attacks continue, Carla invites two college students with an interest in the paranormal to visit her house. After seeing the ghost in action, they agree to help Carla to defeat her invisible attackers. In a nutshell, this movie was creepy, tense, and frightening. But for me, it was research for me and my own experience. I was shocked by what I watched and how these entities were physically raping her just as they had slammed into the door and opened the door and beating on the walls not only at mikes house but at all the many hotels I stayed in. In the hotels, it was as if they knew where I was in the room, be it in the bathroom or the bedroom. They would bang very hard wherever I was. Then all this happened to Mikes. I got so into my investigation I downloaded these apps called Ghost Tube, ghost tube seer, ghost tube S.L.S. and ghost tube vox. I had a few different phones at the time and turned on all the apps at the same time on different phones. The seer app is based on energy frequency, and it will pick up the energy in the room and produce a photo picture. A picture started to appear on my phone, and as it developed slowly, I kept it directed towards Mikes's bedroom outside the sliding door, which faces his backyard. A man with a waspish demeanor on his face with red eyes was what was shown to me.

I then used the regular ghost tube which shows spirits in the shape of a person. The screen showed a few entities in the room, so I started talking to them. One got scared and was trying to hide behind the standing fan in the room repeatedly. I could feel that they were getting anxious and nervous because I saw them and truly believed in their presence. Then one climbed up on me and was humping my face. I was astonished by what I saw. I began to speak to them and asked them questions like what's your name? who are you? Repeatedly. They quickly left the room or house, but I don't know. I even walked through the rest of the house, searching for them, but there was no sign of them anymore. They were no longer showing up on my phone screen. I also had the Ghost Vox app running along with the others. Ghost Vox will pick up what they are saying and speak it out on your phone as well as transcribe the words for you too. It was stating things like possessed, why are you here? Who are you? Devil, and evil. Things that were all associated with hell. I felt like I was getting somewhere with my investigation. I was doing this around 4:30 A.M. It was pouring down rain this morning hard outside as well. I slid the sliding door open just to see how hard it was raining, but I noticed something squatting in the bush in the backyard. It was translucent in its matter but shaped like a person. I am not going to lie, it did make me a little nervous, and I shut the door quickly, but I continued to stare at it.

Which made it kind of creepy, but I don't live in fear.

Fear comes from the devil as well as chaos and confusion so those emotions for me are not part of my character. I have always been fearless, so I laid back on Mike's bed and got comfortable. As I laid there reveling in the paranormal activity and newfound detective skills. something caught my eye out of the peripheral view. I then steered my eyes sight toward the ceiling vent above his bed. That is when I noticed diminutive flies slowly usher out of the slates of the vent into the room and creep on the ceiling. I immediately turned on the ceiling fan light to illuminate what was happening. I began recording this scene which is the same one I had seen in the Amityville Horror movie. I was in awe. This only happens in movies, right but, no it was right in front of my own eyes.

Remember it was almost 5 A.M. by now and pouring down rain outside. So when I heard Mikes's kitchen door to his garage open up, he came barreling into the house, soaking wet and breathing very hard, dragging his luggage behind him. I could tell he was full of stress and anxiety. I had never seen him act like that before. I was feeling as if he knew what I was discovering and investigating. He had never been one to be around traveling in such early morning hours. Even more strange to be out in the torrential rain storm. For some reason, I knew he knew what I was up to but didn't know how I knew he knew lol! I did not mention anything to Mike and went about the day. I did have him drop me off in Turlock and got a room at the Venice Motel, which was not known as the best motel. I noticed that there was no one at the motel except for me. This is the third time I have noticed it like this. This was most unusual because this was a place where a lot of drug addicts hung out and would always be outside in their cars playing music or simply hanging out in the parking lots. This was weird to me. For sure. I was excited to use the new apps I found in this environment. That night I was unpacking my things and cleaning the room up because the maid there was not on the up and up. It was about 2:30 a.m. and I turned on the app as I was doing this. I had the vox app rolling when, all of a sudden, it just kept saying POSSESSED, POSSESSED, POSSESSED for 30 min.

That's when my intuition told me to open my door to check what was outside. Mind you, the last room I was given was next to the dumpster in the building. I directed my eyes to the dumpster and noticed a pair of dirty old shoes lying on the ground in front of it. I thought that it made me look trashy, being that it was so close to my room, so I went over to pick up them up. As I tossed them over the rim of the garbage dumpster, I saw a woman sitting cross legged, facing backwards inside the dumpster. The way I threw the shoes hit her on the head. I apologized to her but got no reaction from her. She sat there motionless and acted as if she did not even realize a pair of shoes had come and whacked her on the head. This made me off set by how I found her chilling in the dumpster like it was the place to be. My reaction to this was to tell her "Girl, gets out of there, please. There are better places to be in this world and it's this dumpster". I repeated this, and she got up and jumped out of the dumpster. I said," God is good, girl, please do not ever get a dumpster like this again". She simply walked away with no comment or stating a word. She merely walked away in a zombie state of lost, empty stare. As far as I could tell was, she looked possessed. I then walked back into my room and shut the door. I was holding my phone and looked at the app and it no longer was saying possessed. The distance from my room and the dumpster from the wall of my room was about a foot. Not far at all. So basically, the energy of the woman in the dumpster was getting picked up by the app. The app alerted me to the fact that there was a demon outside my room. I was so dumbfounded by the encounter I had. So, I turned on Ghost Tube Seer and pointed the camera towards the parking lot, and a picture began to show. The energy it had picked up was demon looking creatures fighting each other right there in the parking lot. A full-blown war in the unseen realm. They were physically wrestling and fighting one another.

I had come across some videos of Jim Carrey acting a little crazy. I had always liked Jim Carrey. All his movies, I simply adored him. But I saw him on a red carpet interview, and he was saying nothing matters, he doesn't exist and a few other things that were kind of strange. I also found some other videos pertaining to him being gang stalked. That's when I knew what was happening to me was happening to many other stars and celebrities, not just regular people out in the world too. Jim Carrey was talking about the penile gland. That's the only thing he ever posted on his Facebook or his YouTube. It was just one thing about the penile gland in our brain. That led me to do great studying Egyptian history. The penile gland is is in our brain, and our penile gland is our third eye. The government has tried to keep all of our third eyes closed with calcium deposits from the water and all the contamination of hormones and pesticides they put into our foods. This keeps us blind from knowing the truth, and Jim Carrey was very helpful in finding my way to the truth. Not only Jim Carrey. Jim Carrey is just an enlightened soul who knows exactly what he's talking about. I see now how intelligent he really is. A lot of celebrities like Martin Lawrence, Dave Chappelle, and Roseanne Barr. Katt Williams. Many many comedians have tried to talk about what's going on in the world. Randy Quaid is another actor I found who was being gang stalked as well. He was on the news trying to tell people how these people were killing actors. He was calling them star whackers. People were portraying him as a crazy person online but I am here to stand on his side even though I am not famous. I was being attacked just like he was. I will testify for any of these actors and comedians to the truth they have been speaking for many years now. To no avail. No one seems to listen or care. But I believe they soon will. These people have also killed many actresses. People that get in their way and anyone they see is competition. They simply get together, make a plan, make a plot and take these people out just for the simple fact of greed or the simple fact that they can't create or Co create with God. Demons can't create anything. So they want to steal our light and take it from us. Those were just a few of the things that I educated myself on during my research. In the dark spirit realm.

I met a man who was a breeder for French bull dogs. I was so in love with this one puppy and asked him if I could have him. I was so surprised that he said yes. After having him in my life. I knew that they were going to make sure I did not have any love in my life. I would not be keeping him long. One afternoon, I had gotten dropped off at a hotel in Ceres CA I had never stayed at. It was around 11 a.m., and couldn't check in until 3 p.m., so Zander and I sat on the grass with all my luggage and things. This day was very hot, and we sat under a tree all afternoon waiting for 3 o check in. 2:45 came around, and a man from the hotel walked all the way across the parking lot just to tell me I was not allowed to stay at his hotel. I tried to explain to the man I had never stayed there before, but he only walked away. I was irritated by this happening because I had no car or no one to call to come pick me up. I mean, literally no one to call. Everyone at this point had jumped shipped on me. They all turned their backs on me. I would have tried to leave by walking, but I had way too much to carry, and with Zander, too would have been too hard to even attempt. I basically was camping there for the night. That evening, the police showed up and tried to make me across the street into a dirt field with fox tails and no trees for shade. I told them I refused to put my puppy in the heat, and I wasn't moving. By this point in my life, I was fed up with the police and the unwarranted harassment constantly being directed towards me. I was rude and stern with these officers and stood my ground. They left, but another set of police showed up to bother me a few hours later. I was so frustrated and upset, but I didn't let them see this in me. This would have been giving them what they were trying to accomplish in the harassment anyway.

Nighttime came, so I spread my blanket out and laid my pillow down, then cuddled up with my Zander. I put Netflix's on and picked a movie to watch on my phone. As we were relaxing, a man came strolling down the sidewalk. My luggage was kind of on the sidewalk, and I started to apologize and sat up to move it. As he passed me, he looked down at me and he had a skin-colored mask on with black eyes. He was wearing a hoody with that creepy mask and looked very dangerous. I immediately went into protection mode. That's when this man demanded that I give him my dog. He said, "give me that dog"! That's when I got up and started bouncing around like a boxer. I was going to fight this man for my baby puppy. I was protecting my puppy. The guy turned and ran away to my disbelief. He ran to an SUV, and they drove right by me and Zander. As they drove by, I was thinking they might shoot me, but they did not. They simply tried to punk me for my dog, then left as fast as they showed up. I held Zander close to my heart and began to cry to him. I told him, "Son you almost got dognapped".

Another incident that occurred was when the Modesto Police Department falsely arrested me and allowed Zander to be taken from me and did not arrest the women who took him after they arrested me. She stole my 5,000-dollar puppy, and they said it was not a crime and told me to take her to civil court. I couldn't even do that because I did not even know this woman's name. I was only given her phone number. When I stayed at another hotel in Modesto. I was waiting for my bank to clear a check to extend my stay. I had already been at this hotel a week. I had to wait outside for the afternoon while waiting at the bank. I had just gotten a cute little French bulldog given to me and was in love with him.

We waited outside all day, playing around and enjoying the sun. A man from another room there came outside and walked by me and targets right on schedule. When this man's eyes met mine as he walked by me, I knew he was directing his threats towards me. Then, some other strange perpetrators came outside of their room with garbs of silky-looking table clothes with ruffles on them. I made a comment to them and said," oh you guys having a wedding in there?" and they came back sharply with 'No, we were astral projecting." Yet another odd bunch of people around me once again. Evening time came, and the woman at the front desk called the police on me. The Modesto police department walked up to me as I was sitting on the curb of the hotel walkway and stated that I was trespassing. and grabbed me up off the ground, threw me against the wall and slapped handcuffs on me. I was crying about Zander and proclaiming my innocence but resisted arrest. Because I once again had done nothing wrong to be arrested for. The police said they could put my dog in the dog pound, or the lady that was holding my dog from this hotel could keep him. I talked to the lady through the window, and she said she would watch Zander, my little baby puppy. He was like my son, and I had grown very close to him. I felt that this lady was being sincere in her help and trusted her when that was the worst thing I could have done. I went to jail and was booked and released with a court date. Somehow, I found a way back to the hotel only to find that the lady had gone and taken Zander right along with her. Mind you, Zander was a 5,000 dollar show dog puppy that someone had given to me. I knew the day he was given to me that I shouldn't have taken him because this cult was not going to allow me to have anything to love. I needed to share my love so badly that I ignored this thought and still took him with me the day I had offered him. I was so distraught and upset that my precious little puppy had been dognapped. The lady at the front desk and said that my friends came and picked him up. This was so crazy to me because I had no friends, let alone someone who I called to come pick him up. Yet another mystery in my book of life. I knew this cult was up to their tricks once again, and I sucked up my tears and anger just as I always had and went on with life. I knew God would handle these people, and that is exactly what I let him do. He was watching all the awful things they had done. These cult members don't believe in God, so of course, there not care about the ramifications or consequences of their horrific actions horrific. But that's how I won, and I won every time these people tried to hurt me. I simply would swallow the pain and go inside. As I internally started speaking to God and my angels, I felt better and comforted. Grace, mercy and love began to surround me. I allowed God to heal my stress and anxiety. I know now I was transmuting the pain into butterflies. I was taking the negative energy being projected on to me and turned it into positive energy by simply not giving my energy to negative behavior. When they start doing the negative things and acting like small children, I would just ignore it. I could not allow immature behavior to even be acknowledged. The minute I gave into this would be the minute they win, and they get what they were looking for out of me. The reaction of my emotions is what they feed on and wait for so that they can harvest it from me. You all need to know that you're in control of your mind and your body. Only you can control what you decide to do and how you react to certain situations that may arise in your life.

So, this is the final and last of the police harassment and false arrests harassment. I was at the Walmart in Turlock, CA. Simply wanted to buy. A hairdryer. I was walking through the store with my music on very quietly. Then, I was approached by one of the employees. Asking me to leave the store because I had been banned from the store. I then. Said OK, I walked out of the store, but as I was walking out of the store, there were five other employees that joined the crusade. I, at this point was very frustrated because it seemed that every time I went shopping, I would be harassed in some shape or form. I didn't get angry, and I simply left the store. But at the last minute I did get pretty close to one of their faces and told them to leave me alone and shut the F up. They called the police. The police came and followed me down the street after I had already left. Then arrested me for theft. I went to jail yet again. So these are the five cases that these people have put upon me falsely, that I've had to deal with for four years. Up until recently as I'm writing this book. I don't wanna talk about what happened to all the cases until I circle around at the end, as I stated previously.

CHAPTER 12

BLACKLISTED

I was forced into living like a vagabond. I was still escorting, but very minimal. I was only doing it to pay for my room and food. Nothing fancy or extravagant. I started to get treated badly by the employees and owners of these hotels and motels. These people were making up petty reasons for me not being able to rent a room with them again. I mean, it was all of them. I could not rent a room from Merced, CA. to Hayward, Ca. I also began to meet warlocks at these hotels. I was like, wow people really think Harry Potters is real. Ok! One specific incident was a man in the room next to mine in Columbia, Ca. He was telling me about how he would travel the world, and it was through his job. I was interested in how and what he did for work that allowed him to travel the world in such a matter. I asked him, what he did for work? He reacted as if he didn't want to answer me and then made a distorted face while snarling at me. He then, bluntly stated "Well, lets' just say we can talk about the end of your life"! I most definitely felt he was threatening me, in the way he aggressively directed the taking my life. I took that as my que, I slammed my hands down on the table and said, "this was real, this was fun, but it wasn't real fun, now I got to go." I walked away back to my room thinking to myself that I need to go to the office in the morning and tell the owners as to what he had said. I knew he was directing threats towards my life but was unsure as to why. I didn't even know this man.

I felt so discombobulated because I knew Harry Potter was not real but didn't understand how I was speaking to an individual who actually was stating he was a practicing a warlock in this modern-day era. I had taken my children to all the Harry Potter movies, and I would think how neat the story lines were. The way the story line seemed so magical, mystical, and fantastical that the human mind can only be lead to believe that the world of warlocks, witches, and wizards are nothing but the mere grand imagination of someone with a very creative and captivating mind.

Many other times. I was told I couldn't stay in hotels. I was banned from hotels. I was harassed while being at the hotel, constantly knocking on my door, the maids knocking on my door, opening my door without my permission. Then my things would get stolen constantly out of my rooms. At one point I. Just kind of gave up on even making plans online because I couldn't make it happen. I was no longer welcomed at any facility, any hotel or restaurant in my town. They would either lock the doors, turn me away, or just simply laugh and walk away without a word to say.

CHAPTER 13

ME VI LA LOCA FAMILIA

In 2022,,,, I called my grandma and asked if I could stay with her. I was blown away when she said yes. My Uncle Byron was living with her in her spare bedroom at the time, and he came to pick me up in the morning from Turlock to bring me to the house in Columbia, CA. He showed up the next morning and picked me up with smiles and hugs. I hadn't had that for so long, but I welcomed it with open arms. I got to the house and was welcomed by my family as if everything was fine. I was happy to be with my grandmother and felt safe for the first time in a long time. Things were going great, and then all of a sudden. The weird behavior of my loved ones that began to occur in a throttled manner directed toward me was undeserved. She had told me if I came home after dark, the door would be locked, so I didn't come back one night and then got yelled at for her leaving the front door open and blamed me for not coming back after she had told me the door would be locked. Then I came back after dark again, and the door was locked, so I climbed through the kitchen window and was met with Frank and my grandma confronting me for climbing through the window. This fight was when I noticed my grandma's face and eyes were different. She did not even look the same to me. This was the night I asked her. What are you? Then she looked at me like confusion, turned around and walked to her room. It was as if I could see the demon that was inside of her. And she knew that I could see her.

The next evening, I was in my room, and they were all three pounding on my bedroom door for no reason. I had the lights off, and I had no TV or radio going, so I just pretended to be asleep. They continued to knock on the door and knock on the door. All of a sudden, I heard the door open. They all crept in very calmly and quietly, but looked really sneakily as they surrounded my bed in one circle, each one on the side of each of the bed. Byron me is at the end, Frank is on the side of me, and my grandmother is on the other side. I laid there as if I was asleep, not breathing very loudly or moving at all. Not wanting to fight with them was my only reason for doing this. Then they all started looking around at each other and startled happiness as if they thought that I'd killed myself. And they were smiling. And then they kept shaking me and saying Shannon, Shannon, Shannon. And I just ignored them. And they were getting happier and happier. I could see the smiles on their face as I looked through the crack of my eyes. I then jumped up and said what? ,They looked so surprised and they all just walked out of my room without saying a word. It was the weirdest experience I've ever had with my family, and it wasn't my family I had the experience with. It was demons inside of each one of my family members.

Today, I stand firm in what I say because it's true. People and family don't act the way that they were acting or continued to act. The entire time I stayed at the house, which was about 3 months. Was nothing but fights, arguments and constant bickering over petty items, things and situations that I couldn't grasp or understand why they were doing it. But today, I know. It was meant to break me down. One night, I was sitting outside. Byron came out and put a gun to my head. He pointed it right at my temple, and I dared not even turn my head to give him the slightest satisfaction that I was scared or threatened in any manner. I simply ignored him, didn't say a word, and just let him be irate in his emotional state, stating that he continued to be in for a good 40 minutes, crying, yelling irately, screaming at me derogatory names, calling me. Poor. I just let it all go. But the next day, I did approach my grandmother and Frank and asked her to please never have that gun put around me ever again and even questioned why there was a gun in the house, to begin with. My entire life, we've never had guns nor even a weapon around any of us, and it confused me as to why there was one now. That day, when I asked her about the gun not being brought out in front of me anymore was when she stated she was going to kill herself with it, and I couldn't understand why she would even make a statement in that manner. I asked her to please don't talk like that. Don't ever say that to me again. And I simply walked upstairs.

One night, I was on the computer upstairs when, all of a sudden, the hall light came on to the stairway. I saw

Frank coming up the stairs very quickly, and he had a huge kitchen knife like the one Michael Myers would use in the Michael Myers Halloween movies. Startled me and scared me to see an old elderly man shaking his hand at me with this huge knife, stating I know someone's up here with you. I know someone's in here. When I saw this and his distraught behavior. I stood up for myself and stated no one's here, Frank, no one's here. I'm here all by myself. I'm just talking to the computer and laughing. Calm down and put the knife away. It took him a minute after he was frazzled, and then he walked down the stairs again. The next day, my grandmother sat me down With Frank on the couch. She stated quote. Frank has something to tell you. I said OK, and he said I'm sorry, Shannon. But I didn't feel a true sorry coming from him. Another situation that happened while I was there was when I had to go to court down in Modesto, and they came and picked me up. But all the times before, Frank had kept telling me I talked too much, that I never shut up, that I needed to shut up. And so this time, I brought my headphones and wore them the entire time. As we were leaving the courthouse, I put my headphones on to satisfy him, and so I didn't have to argue or listen to his mean, cruel words. My grandmother, I suppose, was talking to me and asking me for directions because she started yelling and screaming on a very busy road. And I've never seen her act in such a manner to where she was yelling so high. Only dogs could hear that tone. She got out of the car on a very busy road, and it scared me that somebody was going to hit her ,so I told her to get in the car and quit being weird. She got back in the car, and Frank turned around and had his fist turned up at me as if he was going to hit me in the face. I immediately turned on my video camera on my phone and started recording. I alerted Frank as to the video going so that I would have proof of the violence that he was directing toward me. I could see him getting so mad and shaking inside his hands, and his body was vibrating from anger for no unpainted reason. The entire drive back was Very uncomfortable. I got to the house and went upstairs immediately. All these things kept happening, but I just couldn't see it because I didn't want to see it. I was just happy to have my family back. I didn't care how they were acting. I thought I could change them. I thought I could help them. What I see now is that there was no helping them. They were no longer my family. They had sold their souls long ago.

I was still seeing Mark, the youngster from Atwater. I had Grown to believe we were close and we were dating. At this point, I was living so far away. And I was falling in love with Mark. I stopped escorting, I told all my clients I had quit, and I was only going to be seeing Mark from that point on. Mark would come up and see me occasionally. And I began to trust him very much. I had just opened a new account on a sight called Booty Calls. I was receiving so many messages that I asked Mark to help me answer all my messages. I gave him my profile name and password. I didn't realize he was going to do me dirty at all. A few days later, I got on the site and looked at my profile. I then saw that my picture had been changed to another woman, and my name had been changed as well to Horny Delia. I instantly contacted Mark and confronted him about this discovery. He acted as if it was no big deal and blew it off as a mere joke. He then called me a few days later and admitted to me that he had gotten a cash app card in my name and was getting men off my account to send him thousands of dollars without my knowledge. He then gave 500.00 dollars. He would make fake appointments and not show up because he was not me, or he would send other girls to pretend they were me. I couldn't stay mad at him and accepted his apology. We even went on a trip to Angels Camp for the night. It made me feel very special. He and I did not see the evil intentions he had directed towards me. I even introduced him to my grandmother and to Frank, and my grandmother's response was, wow, how does a nice young man like that fall in love with you? And how could he even love you? I had all intentions of being loyal to Mark. And only Mark. We were even talking about marriage and baby names.

One day, Frank and taken me to the store, and I threw a napkin out on the ground. Then I reached back in the car to grab my purse, and that's when Frank punched me in the face. I yelled at him and told him to leave, and I was not getting the car with him again. He drove off and left me at the store. I then bought a drink ,walked into the next parking lot area, and found a rock to sit on. That's when I saw my grandma's car go by and then came flying into the parking lot, heading right in my direction. That's when my uncle Byron hit me with a car and pinned me up against a rock for about 2 minutes as he was yelling at me verbatim, "we all want you dead, grandma, Frank, your dad, Austin, Hannah, Tawnie, Melisa, William, Kevin, Brandon, uncle Steve and aunt Debrah." This was basically everyone in my family and everyone in my inner circle. I was shocked at the words that this very close family member who I loved deeply was speaking to me. I responded to his discerning words with, "Oh you want me dead, ok then I am going to live for 200 years now'. He then sneered his teeth with a demonic grin, pointed at me and then punched the ceiling of the car. I immediately hoped on the bus and went to the sheriff's department and made a police report. The police did nothing in return on my behalf. I was so let down by the justice system once again. That night I packed up my things and called Mark to come pick me up. We then went down into Columbia, Ca. and got a hotel room where I had met the warlock. Mark dropped me off and left. After he left, the couple next door was fighting loudly, and I heard the man getting violent and hitting the woman. I called the front desk to alert him to this abuse. He came and knocked on the door of their room next door. I was listening to the conversation, and he only gave them a warning to stop fighting. The next night, Mark came to stay the night with me, and we were being sexual together. and around 1:00 A.M. the owner came and knocked on the door and asked us to leave because I was having orgasms. I couldn't believe how I was being asked to leave, but the domestic violence that occurred the night prior was left unresolved. I threw a fit and packed up the car. Mark then took me to Merced, and we slept in the car. The next morning, he dropped me off in Turlock. Mark understood I needed to do what I needed to do after being asked to leave my family again.

I met up with a new client at a hotel. This new client I met up with then got his phone out and asked me if the ad he was showing me was my profile ad. I replied, 'Yes, that's me, and that's my profile". He sat back in his car seat and said, " why did you rob me with your black boyfriend at the El Captain Hotel"? I was completely thrown off by his statement and didn't even know what the El Captain Hotel was. I looked at him with disgust and was offended by what he was accusing me of. I told him," First of all if you think I did all the horrible things to you, why do you want to hang out now? That's weird, and I am not going into that room with you. I look back now and think he was probably going to get revenge on me for something one of my copycats was out here doing. Just another example of when I listened to God's direction to save me. This was when I decided I did not care about escorting and all my clients. I gladly handed over my clients. I felt if these people could turn you away from that easily, it's your loss because I know who I am, and it's your loss, not mine. I knew God was telling me in his own way this is not your path. This is not who you are.

My sister was pregnant once again, and I then I never saw the baby or ever knew what happened. She would not talk about it. She had gotten pregnant at least 12 times I knew of without any baby to speak of after these pregnancies. Around town, people were calling her the black widow. She had four of her men who had been murdered. One died in a car accident. I always stuck up for her because, at the time, I did not see my sister capable of being a killer. I was so gullible for trusting her. I just loved her so much that I could not see the truth of her character.

I decided to stay in Turlock at the Turlock in Motel for a few days. This was the night I showed up at Christians's house, and he said they can't hear us with the water running and proceeded to give me a lesson on the creatures. I went back to my motel room and turned the water on to test his theory. I also turned on the record video button and set my phone in the window just to record the cars going by. The crazy thing is I did record something out of this world. Between the building and the fence across the street is the Venice motel's backyards. It's a wide-open space. I recorded huge bright lights coming from the ground up and shooting off into the morning sky. It went on for hr or so. It also showed huge towering black figures walking back and forth in the silhouette of the fie orb balls. I even put it on my youtube channel. The next day, I went to show it to some guys I knew named George and Sarge. I decided to show Sarge, and Sarge next spoke to me again. Then, the next time I saw George. George could not even look at me without puking. I was concerned for him, and all he could say it's not my fault they shouldn't have done it. Then, go back to almost vomiting. When I was checking out of the motel, I was waiting to decide what I was going to do. I was chilling on the sidewalk with my things when all of a sudden, the owner of the hotel begins to spray raid on the bushed right by me. The wind was blowing pretty good as well. I nicely asked him if he could not spray me with his chemicals, when he responded by calling the police. The police then showed up, stating I was impeding pedestrians and I had to leave. I curiously asked if they would watch my stuff as I went down the street to get my mother's van. I had no idea if she would help me at all. I did not speak to my mother all the time and did not like to ask her for things. When I started to leave my things on the sidewalk. The police then said they were going to take my things because now it was abandoned property. I simply walked as fast as I could down the street. To my surprise, my mother was there and said yes, she'd take me to get my things. When we pulled up, the cop was still being rude and trying to perpetuate a fight when there was none to be had. At one point, the cops went over to my mother's driver's window, and she told him my name. I asked her if she had just told that cop my name, and I was met with a blank stare and a wicked smile that she had turned up on her face. She did not even turn her head to look at me. Solid cold evil I saw in my own mother. My mother had recently gotten back with an ex of hers she had been broken up with for around 13 years, to, just like my father. Estaban was a nice Spanish man who I thought was somebody else until his mask fell off, to. This was the day my mother told me something about herself. She finally admitted to me she knew what was happening to me. She told me when it happened to me, and I did not want to tell anyone because I did not want everyone to think I was crazy. My mind was blown knowing that she knew this whole time the atrocities that were being done to me and did not help me. She just sat back and watched as well was, helping me to think I was going crazy.

I was upset but did not let her know I was. I just called Mike and asked him to come get me. When Mike came he said he was leaving town for the weekend and dropped me off at his house. When I walked into his kitchen, I found a random cell phone in his kitchen table basket and thought cool, maybe I could use this phone because this cult did not know about this phone. They always monitored and hacked into everything of mine. Phones, emails, and text messages were always monitored by them. They would retrieve my messages and such before me. I popped my SIM card in, and omg. I was blown away at how fast I got to set up my profile. I used to take 3 hrs sometimes trying to get things to download or even to not say error. It was so cool. I was using a phone like it's meant to be used fast. Not like dial-up. The next day came, and mike saw I had the phone. I asked him If I could have it, and then the next day, the phone was blacklisted as stolen. They didn't want me to use a phone without their involvement. He probably got in trouble for allowing me to find it. Loose end. Another cool thing about Mike was to perfect was he would let me drive his truck sometimes. One day, I drove out to Oakdale to do some recon. I went by a previous client's home and started talking with his roommate Slash girlfriend. She was doing the loud vacuum harassment with the cars running. The whole shebang. I had never mentioned any of the crazy things that were going on in my life to this woman. So it was odd for her to say out of the blue. "I knew this was coming long before you were born, and if you would just be good to them, they'll be good to you". I asked her before I left if they were going to eat me. Thinking about cannibals, she snickered like a sexual creep. The statement long before I was born stuck with me, rolling in my mind. This was the day I knew for sure this was part of. The of the spirit world. God's angels and ancestors were guiding me, and he downloads kept coming to me. I just kept flowing in the direction I was pointed to investigate. I began to research Cern and the opening of the Switzerland Tunnel. From the tunnel opening, I was led to articles and stories about the tunnels under all these towns and cities people that the masses can't even begin to understand. These real issues that are most definitely right under our feet. These tunnels are to keep the trafficking of children and sex slaves to be unseen by the natural world's eyes. God told me about these, and I am here to tell you all He heard my cries and came with his vengeance when I called upon my Lord. People are mad at me that I have the favor of the Lord. I am so sorry you feel that way. Know I would never wish any harm like you have directed to me. I free you all of the guilt. I am aware that you were all tricked by the master of lies. I won't forget the lessons. They were scares I am proud to wear. I wore them for the others who were afraid to stand up. I wanted the wasted time and weird illusions to stop. I knew I was not living in my truth. Until The truth came upon my life like a thief in the night. This was the video evidence that I had come across of something so out there I cannot explain it to you. I can only stand before you today, stating my truth. Mike had known I was seeing a few clients when he left for the weekend. I actually did and followed through with the few I did choose to give my time to. When Mike came home, he asked me 'why I did not see anybody?" I laughed and said what are you talking about. I did see, and I counted them out. Mike says. Oh well, I have a video of you opening the door on the ring doorbell video. But nobody is coming in or leaving. It was only me opening the door and talking to the air. I was not talking to the air. I physically had dates that came for my services I had sexual relations with. I was astonished as I watched the ring video, which was evidence of the ghost people that I had been intimate with that day. I was kinda of set back by this proof. I could not die. I was there with real people, but the real people were not even on the video when I opened the door. It was only me. I also had noticed in mikes shower vent. It was a video camera that would blink when I would move? It had a green blinking light that would flash. I knew he was recording me. I sometimes would just wave. I just wanted them to know I knew they were watching me. I stopped spending as much time at Mikes.

I had made a vow I was not going to put ads out ever again, and I was done with these warlocks trying to use me and hurt me. I was not into the occult; I was just into God's Word and aware of how valuable my soul is. I needed to start protecting my energy and was working on helping my soul get better without them. I needed to leave the entire scene. I dropped off. I still all the copycats and weird things going as well. I gave them Horny Holly. I did not care about what they thought was going to destroy me. I was well aware God was telling me the wrong direction. A burglar is not going to break into an empty house. He knows when it's worth it. He may want to fight for my soul when I don't have to fight because the battle is not my own. I know I beat the devil by just letting go. I definitely got God's message about the direction I was heading in. A lot of not caring what others were doing but focusing on what I am doing. Not wondering what some ones got on their plate. If you always have your eyes on someone else's plate, then you can't be open to your own blessing and the path God had intended for you. Your blessing that might even be bigger than the person you're jealous of. I was only seeing Mark and Fabian. I stopped seeing everyone but. I had used the last of my money on a air b and b. I did not want to go around Christians's house because I was constantly being monitored by monitoring spirits. No talking or conversations, just 2 of them sitting like zombies, like listening to my thoughts and trying to do some kind of mental magic on me. I knew when they would be doing their rituals watching, and I would just observe and almost laugh inside to myself because I could see every move they would make. I was ten times as fast at this point. I was always a step or two ahead. Ahead of what, I was not completely sure, but I had the tools God had given me, and I stuck to what I knew. I began to sleep down on the train tracks on a little fake skin bearskin fur rug. I was on the busiest street in Turlock. I was on Golden State Blvd without care in the world. I was bound and determined to prove to these people that I did not need their dirty money. I knew if God took care of the birds, he would surely take care of me. My mom and estiban were a few blocks down, and I had thought my mom would not mind at least letting me shower and eat at her house. I had nowhere else to go. I hated to go ask her for help. I figured that she had never really done anything for me my entire life. She shouldn't be helping me. I pinch as an adult. Maybe thought I'd be treated like a daughter. AHH. Yeah, that was not the case at all. My mother lived in a little RV. trailer park on Almond Ave. My sister, who is 10 years younger than me was always running the streets, and I rarely saw her. Then, she began being there every day. She was even given a bed in RV. for her and her little dog, she had many years. Matter of fact, my sister ended up stealing my 5,000 puppies and sacrificing him as an altar. My mother's response was you know you can't have nice things like that. But I came back with wow, but Cassie can. Her little baby girl puppy was some kind of expensive tea-up chihuahua. I was definitely made to feel unwanted by any and all. I did come across one of my mom's neighbors named Mark as well. He was an older gentleman who I thought was pretty solid. My sister had just been a part of stealing an expensive Harley motorcycle right out of his drive way. As he was telling me how he thinks my sister was involved I could not deny the fact that my sister is always involved in taking things that do not belong to her. What's even crazier is the nickname the ton has given her. They call her the black widow. I never allowed people to talk ill of her name in front of me about her being a murderer. I always stuck up for her and never even thought of my sister being such an evil, wicked thing as they were saying she was. I see today the true evil that can be sparked by the fuel of the lies and seeds of deception. One of the other neighbors next to my mothers r.v. would always yelling fuck you, Cassie, you're a witch. And I would think he was just calling her a witch. Then he was calling Esteban a warlock. Estaban even told me, "I am the warlock, the man with the money," and he would slap his pockets. This was the first I had heard anything bout him being a warlock or Harry Potter. No clue. Until one day, I was hanging out at my mother's, trying to cool off from the summer heat. I never knew Esteban hated me like he did. He was pacing back and forth and said pinchie poota. And look me right in the eye. My mom was telling me I was causing problems for her and that I needed to go. Always pinie poota, though. I didn't know what he was calling me at the time, but I do now. Then, one day, he kept trying to get me to meet a guy. I didn't want to go, and he was pissed that night. I slept outside under a tarp with the cockroaches. The next morning, I knocked on the R. V. door to use the restroom. When I entered the r. v. Estaban was cooking chorizo and eggs at the stove. He was not just cooking,. He was full-blown, crying tears of sadness and regret. He turned around and begged for my forgiveness and apologising to me. He said he was sorry, Shanon, and I am sorry, Shanon. My sister even began to act weird too. She would make these bi dinners, but no one was eating them but me. The thing is, I was unaware my sister had been poisoning my food. I thought she so lovingly made me.

I ended up sleeping in the bushes off Highway 99. I had found a little spot that was carved out and somewhat of a shelter. It was summertime, and it was at the top peak of the gang stalking. I was going to hang myself inside that bush one night, but I woke up the next day. Put myself together and went about my day. I kept going when I was not full even here. I was going through my own dark night of the soul. I was looking inside at me. I was not focusing on the pain and obstruction placed on me like chains of emotional venom. Like they expected they expected me to be thirsty and weak. I was to follow the line, but it would all go away if I would just surrender to the wishes of their demands. I would be better off. I stood ten toes down. I began speaking about what I was going through daily to everyone. I quickly realized everyone around me knew what was going on except for me. It is an awful feeling to feel out of all the emotions I went through on my journey to peace and enlightenment. I was done escorting and done giving myself to random people just for a good time in bed. Staying between my mom's and the train tracks, I balanced my day. My nights were mom, Cassie and Esteban all koozie in the R.V. with air on and chilling. I am left outside on the ground with cock roaches crawling all over me, head to toe, and cats everywhere. In the heat. I was shocked by the treatment of my mother and sister. I did meet the neighbor Mark, and it became very clear Mark knew about the weirdness, too. He would always tell me to be quiet and I did not know what I was talking about. Until this one sunny day, he sat me down and said you know Shannon, I really love you and think you deserve to be happy. You've never gotten to be happy, and you, out of all people, deserve it. He also said he had never heard anyone talk about it the way I did. He said even if it means we're the slaves now. You deserve to be happy. I thanked him for his kind words. He also became one of the community members who were an admitted demon in a human suit. Mark said yes, they live inside, and he showed me the bump in his gut area. Another man I met who said he was on the good side of the Luciferians, which was the most confusing sentence I had to ever tried to wrap my mind around. Don't know how that's even a thing. Right. This man said his demon was inside him, too and showed me his bump in his small gut. It was the same bump, just different because Mark was a big guy, and this Luciferian guy was a tiny little weakling.

I was still seeing Mark from Atwater on a regular basis, and I never thought he was truly on the hater team; he was behind my back. I was not sure what he was up to, but I always tried to hide out from him, but somehow, he would always find me. I was testing things at the end of the game. I was perfecting my skills of intuition. I was almost testing myself in the process. I was aware I have power, and I was awakened to it. I had Mark come to see me when I was Mike's in the evening. We had not seen each other in months. Months prior, he had gone on vacation with his family to Lake Tahoe for the fourth of July. He was arrested at his home in Atwater. He was charged with Robbery ,breaking into the homes of women and sexually assaulting their feet in their sleep. I found this out when God told me to turn on the news a few days after the fourth as I looked at the screen only to see Markie looking back at me with the shattered shame of an inmate photo. I knew things were off when he didn't show or call me for months. If I had not of seen the news report, I would never have known anything about his arrest. Months went by, and we got together to discuss things. I explained to him I knew about the broken contract with the devil and it's over, and there was nothing you could do. I asked him if I was a witch, and he exclaimed with all his passion that I was not a witch and told me to never call myself a witch again. He said I was an earth angel and that they should not have done it to me. He just kept saying you kept telling me I was going to get in trouble, and I did. You wished this upon me, he said. He said repeatedly he should never have done it. What it was, I am still not fully positive, but I do know it was about my demise and my destruction. You can't stop what God had His hands on. I am the creator's creation, not the faker's fake station. Things got twisted for you all when I turned my pain into my purpose. Knowing that you have nothing to do with how I survived and how I overcame things you could never even attempt to conquer. Mark from the trailer park was not feeling well and said that I could stay the nights instead of sleeping out on the train tracks, but I did not trust him or anyone at this point. I was on guard with the world. That's when my sister began to come to Marks and try to turn him away from being my friend. I was finally experiencing it first-hand. I simply acknowledged the hate directed towards me by my sister, and began to pay more attention to her behaviors and activities. I was given a sign that she had been coping me and was going to set me up for a crime I did not do. I immediately knocked on my R.V. door only to see God's warning was correct. My sister Cassie dressed in a yellow tank top and jeans overall. And the day before, she had given me a wig that looked just like her hair color and haircut style. I am glad I did not wear it out anywhere. I demanded Cassie explain her outrageous copy cat behavior and demanded her to stop the weird shit. Cassie was even participating in the noise harassment with the loud tools and banging and stuff right by my head when I would sleep outside the R.V. One afternoon, Cassie showed me a text message from my daughter Hannha to her 2 years prior. It was a message saying, who's this bitch, and why is her I.D. in my driveway. My daughter was holding the picture of Lizze's I.D. in photo on the message. This meant that Lizz had been in Twain Harte at my father's house. I don't know why Cassie showed it to me, but she did.

She would smile in my face and then was talking crap

behind my back. I could not understand why. I had always loved her, but this was getting out of control. Mark, the neighbor guy at my mom's r.v. the park had even seen Cassie as a hater when it came to me because he saw I was not doing anything to anyone to deserve slander being committed upon my name. Mark had told me he had a lady friend named Brenda who could get me a cash paying job where I could make the honest day's pay by cleaning businesses and houses with her. I had heard his offer a few times but pushed it off to the side of my mind. Until Mercy retrograded under the moon, and I began to awaken. I was sitting on the dirty train tracks broke and broke down. Then the saying from A.A. hit me upside the head. It said to get up and do something different. The definition of insanity is doing the same thing over and over, expecting different results. I thought of Marks's girlfriend who could get me a legit job. I called Mark, and he gave me her number. I called her, and we set up a time for later that afternoon. I got picked up by her. We went to clean a kitchen at a trucking company. She also told me how she loved the Lord too. I thought it strange that while we were cleaning she was on the phone just trying to get another church member to peace. I definitely had my entas up and guarded. How could someone be of God and sit around and gossip about their church member like she had been doing? I let it slide and went with her to her church in Keys, Ca. I was ready for God to come into my life fully. I wanted to show the world who I ran to when things were too harsh on me. I ran to the church. I will tell you the very next day. Everything changed. The laughing had stopped, and everyone had fear in their eyes. I noticed right away.

How things were no longer funny, and something was going well for me. I saw I had the upper hand but was not quite sure how much of an upper hand. I could tell people were going out of their way not to mess with me now. Finally. I felt a breakthrough in this war. I stood ten toes down and still remained loyal to my Father through all the trials and tribulations, exasperated on purpose intended to smother me with stress and problems. I went out to church a few times with Brenda and Mark until I realized they were not really going to church but going as a front for the enemy. A way to lead me from finding me. I was at Brenda's one afternoon after we had gone to church. I noticed she had put on an interview with a star seed. I had already in my research had watched this particular video, and I found I resonated with the things the woman was proclaiming happening in her life. When I heard Brenda say oh, star seeds aren't real, this lady is crazy. I boldly stood up and said If you think she's crazy why are you watching her. I had to go. I was aware star seeds are real, and I was not going to argue. I simply walked out and left it that. I never felt comfortable around Brenda again. I felt her twisted projection being directed my way, full of more lies to cover all the other lies previously told. Band-aids that can only be a temporary fix. Not a true friend, just a sample person. One serving friend sent in only to distort my truth and my awakening. I was still sticking to my guns. I was detaching from people left and right. If you were playing games, I had to let you go. I ran I to George and explained to him how awful it was to know everyone around me knows what's going on and I didn't. And it's my life. I asked him how he would feel. I asked him to put himself in my shoes. I asked Georgie to answer one question, and he agreed. I asked him George, where are you from up there and pointed to heaven. Or are you from down there and pointed to hell. He looked very disappointed and with puppy dog eyes with, almost a innocent. ,He looks me right in the eye and points his thumb downwards, claiming this is where he is from. I witnessed him and his mask falling off. I knew I had done something big in the spirit realm but how big I still don't know yet. I believe that my faith manifested freedom from oppression for all. I am not alone. I am part of a collective. Something much bigger than you and I. A source of knowledge and being able to be one of the only few who will get to experience greatness when everyone said she could not do it. I will be the name on their minds as they try to sleep at night. I will haunt them with the Holy Ghost and my ancestors. I only wanted the universe to do what the universe does. I understood that it is alive, and it is here to balance out the wrongs. It is here. to create change for a better future. Congratulations to the authentic ones who made it to this next level of life. High vibrational beings across the planet are doing what God has put us here to do. We are no longer being held back by the oppressors of domination over our joy and directing our happiness narrative. We, as a collective, strive for the betterment of humanity in order to ensure a true purpose and a common way of peace in all things. Will and can,, in fact, someday be a reality we can live as the Father first intended for each of us.

I had gotten the little piece of my settlement money from my sexual harassment, and I stayed at the Hampton

Suites off the 99 for a few weeks. One evening, when I came back to my room, I was bumped in the shoulder by a random woman who then tried to act as if I had started something with her. When I recognized exactly the same old situation happening again, I knew the police were going to be involved. Without a doubt. Of course, what do you know, hotel security comes banging on my hotel room door. I had to drawback my curtains to see what was going on in the parking lot. I had been staying on the top floor and could see the real police were still out front by their cars. They had sent the security up to harass me because they knew they did not have any legal crime to charge me with. Nothing to prove I was breaking any laws. The security eventually left, but then I went outside, and my card was no longer active to use to get back into the building. I knew this was retaliation for not getting arrested. I then walked around and was greeted by the hotel staff as a group. I was then asked to pack up my things and leave the hotel immediately. They all followed me back to my room and stood by watching my every move as I packed my things. I was gathering my things, but at the same time, I was being calm and declaring to them all that just because your parents are born into this, and you're born into this, does not mean you have to be like them. You don't have to make me leave, guys. I know you can control what you're doing right now. But in reality, you can't because you're told to behave this way or face the conse-quences. I just kept saying, you don't have to be like ,the people. You can do it too. I was actually shocked when one of them responded with a face of guilt and asked me, "well, how did you do it?" I pointed straight up to heaven and declared loud as can be with God. I did it with God. I was excited to see I had gotten to one of them. I had rolled all my things outside the hotel and had to walk right by the police, that had gathered there a crime scene had happened. I walked right up to one of them and told him " screw you and your illuminate bullet. He responded to my rejection with, "Hey, it's not too late to join." He put his hands out like he had a great offer for me by joining. I had run into David and was kind of glad to visit with him. Until we were having a conversation about him and me opening a church together, but He was explaining to me that I would have to bow down and pray to his aunt what-soever. I was going to pee when I stood up and whipped quickly. I pulled my britches up in anger. I rejected all he had said and, stood in my beliefs and told him I will never pray to another God but my God. That's when he grabbed me up by the throat and choked me harder. He then slammed my head up against the wall, and was continuing the pressure upon my windpipes. I was worried he was going to actually do it. He released me, and I gathered myself together and dissolved from the abuse I walked away, step by step, and as I was leaving, he was yelling at me, but were The Grove but were the Grove. I told him I don't care. I am not about that. A few weeks after, he treated me so lawful. I received a phone call from David. He was in guilt and full of remorse. He apologised to me and said what he did was wrong and he never should have done it. I forgave him and let it go.

I was only going to my mom's to spy on them all. I mostly observed my family's behaviors. It had been over with Mark. He was facing some time for touching those women's feet and was not interested in seeing me anymore. I did catch him coming to see my sister one night, but I just let it all go. Like I said, you can't let others behavior tell you who you are. If they are a jerk to you, then that's their loss. Not yours. I always told myself I was a good person and I did not deserve the harsh treatment I had been getting. My mother would sit for hours just staring at the tent I was staying in. I could see her perfectly through a crack between the zipper. She would sit with her jaw dropped to the floor., and I was shocked. I was in her RV. one night. I had just shaved my private area and was a little itchy. I slightly itched my higher leg area when my mom suddenly said,"? What you got crabs or something. Stop doing that. Esteban is watching you. I looked down the hall, and there he was ,lying on the bed, watching me. I walked over to the microwave and started to warm up something when she said," he's always watching you" I knew I had done something big. I definitely noticed no one was laughing anymore. That had all stopped. I told them over and over again that I was going to have the last laugh. And look at who got the last laugh. People can't say I did not warn them or try to lead them in the right direction. I really tried to warn everyone. I was only met with disregard for my truth and mostly cocky attitudes filled with laughter and doubt.

I was still getting my mail at my grandmother's house still and had Mike to drive me to pickup my mail in Columbia. He agreed and drove me up to retrieve it. The day prior, on youtube, a video popped up about an angel tarot reading. I listened to the message and all the crazy stuff they were saying. I agreed and resonated with what the message was except for one part. She had said I was going to receive some unexcepted money. Which was something I totally knew was not going to happen. The crazy part of this story is when Mike took me to get my mail. There was, in fact, a letter and a check from the unemployment office for 5,000 dollars. I was notified that the funds I was due were stolen, and here is my payment. So basically, my family stole my funds from my unemployment, which is why, years prior, I had received that letter saying I had funds still, but I was not allowed access to them. It was making some sense now. Mike and I were blown away by the prediction of the angel reader. I was shocked to find out my family did really steal from me in such a sneaky legal manner. I learned right then and there that my family was definitely involved with higher-ups in society in order to accomplish this theft. I was also concerned as to why my father was getting all my back child support. I would not ever get a check. They were all going in my father's name and given to him. They had their hands in every aspect of my life concerning money.

I had Mike drop me off back at my mom's r.v. When I entered her r.v. she had said she was going to go to the hospital because of her c.o.p.d. She said I could stay while she was gone. I was happy to stay and not have to spend my money on a hotel room. She was gone for 4 days, and I stayed with Estaban. Things were ok while she was gone. The day she came back from the hospital, she sat next to me, placed her hand on my knee and turned to look me dead in the eye. I asked her how she was feeling. She replied," I feel much better now. The nurses put a demon in me, and I feel much better now." Then she removed her hand and faced forward again. I just continued to rub her back and said, "That's good, Mom" with a strange look on my face. My mom was even scared to sleep in her bed. She would say, "look back there, you see it. Every time I get in my bed, something grabs me." I did not see anything when I would look in her room. She began to sleep on the front bed made out of the dining area. I was not feeling comfortable at Mom's, so I walked down to Marks trailer. I visited with Mark a while, and he said just come stay at his house. I packed up my things and stayed with Mark. Mark also had a girl named Lizzie who would stay with him sometimes, but she moved her things in right before I could. I did not mind I simply kept sleeping on the train tracks, getting rooms, and staying with Mike. I did not want to stay at my mom's. I started to see the depth of my family's situation. I felt the hate being directed toward me without hesitation. I needed to know why, and I was determined to figure out what was going on. One afternoon,, I got a sneaking feeling that they were up to something at my mom's. I walked directly over to the RV. and knocked on the door. My sister answered the door with a nasty attitude. I stepped into the RV. and immediately noticed my mom's phone sitting on the countertop. When they were not looking, I grabbed the phone and put it in my pocket. I needed to know what was on her phone. I needed to get my proof. I was thrilled as I stood there with the phone in my pocket. I was thinking, finally, I am going to get some information. True information like emails and text messages is real evidence. I backed out of the trailer and said my goodbyes. I hurriedly walked back to Mark and, turned off the phone, and hid it under Marks's bed mattress. I then heard a loud pounding knock on his trailer door. I knew it was my sister. I begged Mark not to open the door for her. She was only gin to start drama. That's when she started yelling, "Give me mom's phone." Lizzie was not even friends with Cassie, but there she was, standing behind her as back up when I peeked out the window. Mark opened the door, and that's when the police walked up on the scene. They asked me to come outside and instantly placed me in handcuffs. Lizzie and my sister went into the trailer and immediately found the phone with find my device, even though it was turned off. I was blown away that they found it. I had only intended to get some kind of peace of mind off her phone. I was then placed under arrest and put in the back of the police car. As I was sitting in the police car, another officer cane on his car speaker and asked, "Where is the Rosicrucian"? Another officer responded with, "she's in the back of my partner's car"! I had done a little research on the Rosicrucian. I knew right when I heard the conversation, it was part of the secret society beliefs. I was taken to jail and arrested for theft. I could not believe that I was once again arrested by my own family. I do admit I took her phone, but I only took it to investigate what my mother was up to. Not to steal it. I was going to put it right back after I thoroughly examined it. I had found out for sure that my sister was, in fact, a witch by her own statements. Then, I found out my mom's boyfriend Estaban is a an admitted warlock. My family was full of demons, witches and warlocks. It's a harsh reality to learn that people really are out here in the world doing spells and black magic. Not just any people but my own people had been playing in the dark arts for my entire life and I had no clue. A few weeks after this, Lizz was found dead in Marks's trailer. She died from Fentinaol. I believe she was sacrificed because they couldn't kill me. I have no proof, just a hunch. My mom's neighbor Mark had gotten sick and told me I could stay in his trailer while he went to the hospital. My sister had been parked right outside his trailer with somebody else's mini trailer. Before he left, I had asked him to tell her to leave because I didn't feel comfortable with her being there. She refused to leave, and he was sick, so I didn't wanna push the subject. He went to the hospital, where they admitted him. That night. As after I got out of the shower, I was standing in the living room, and I heard sparks from underneath the trailer. Sparks like fire or wires popping and then all of a sudden bang. Flames started coming from the bottom of the trailer and smoke and fire, and I screamed, and I ran out, and who was standing outside, there was my sister. I yelled at her. I said what did you do? And she just stood there holding her hands out, saying Illuminati, Illuminati. And doing the Illuminati sign. She tried to burn me up in a fire at Mark's trailer. She tried to set me on fire that night. When the fire department came, she wouldn't even let me talk to them, so she overtook the conversation and said she was in charge. I didn't wanna argue or fight. I just went back into the trailer. I stood there very concerned as to my sister's mental state of being as she had just tried to murder me in Mark's trailer. I stayed with Mark for a few weeks after he came home from the hospital, and he began to act weird, too. He would turn on his devil music very loudly and sit on his bed and monitor me. I could tell the low vibrational demons were watching me through him. I would put my plugs earplugs in so the beat of the music couldn't affect me. I then left and started staying in an abandoned house. I did not want to enter the house, so I stayed in the water heater room. It was small and cramped, but at least I had somewhere to stay.

One day, I went to stay at Mike's house, and he admitted they weren't laughing anymore, Shannon. I was so happy to get this confirmation, and it was not just in my head. He said it's not about causing me issues or problems it's about disrupting my life. If I was going to cause them problems, they were going to cause me problems. Even though Mike would talk about them and what was happening to me, he never gave up real information. I was left to fit the pieces together. I added all the compiled evidence I had experienced and found together and realized my own family had tried to get me to kill myself. They made me a pawn sacrifice. I was left to the wolves to die. My awareness of what they were doing had broken some kind of massive spell they had placed on their coven. People began to see that God was real. I turned people from this cult and helped wake up a lot of people to the truth. The truth of God and the Holy Spirit. No one believed that God would come and save me. Just because they did not believe it doesn't mean I was going to give up my faith.

I started noticing cars parked on the streets with cobwebs attached and filthy. I could tell something was up. These abandoned cars were up and down every street. I was concerned as to what was happening. Then, at night, when I would go on walks, I would not see another soul driving or outside. The streets were completely empty every night.

I went to visit Christian and arrived at his beautiful home to find it in disarray. The entire kitchen was a complete mess, and the floor was covered in glass. I then saw that his windows were blown out of the kitchen, and his stove was gone. I asked him what happened, and he said he was making GHB, and it blew up and blew the windows out. I instantly knew it was his karma. We had a visit and talked about what had been happening to me. He became very agitated with me and, in frustration, said to me," ok, I get it, but you're still alive and we're just not going to talk about it anymore, ok Shannon". I was not going to accept that. I said, 'Christian, you all tried to kill me". He was smoking GHB at the time and sat back on his bed with a distorted high on his face from the drugs he was using, and he said, "where all the hoes" and I said " Christan they either moved or died" He was upset with my response and said "NOOOOO" and threw a fit like a toddler. I left his house and went to stay in his rec room at the trailer park he owned. After all the times I needed a place to stay, when all the drama was going on, he never would allow me to stay. But after I had broken the curse on my life, he was all about helping me. I was waiting for my check from my attorney and had plans of leaving town. My check was mailed to my grandmother's house, and I had no way to get it. I had to ask my grandmother to come down to Turlock to bring it to me. My grandmother is also sick with cancer and did not want to bring it, but the next day, my father and grandmother brought it to me. They showed up complaining and making statements about my looks. They were doing their normal dismantlement of my self-esteem. I just took my check and told them I would walk to the bank. I did not want to be around their negative behavior. This happened to be a Saturday, so I had to wait one more night. At least, that was what I thought. I ended up taking a Lyft to 6 different towns and 6 different banks to cash the check. It took me a week to finally find a Bank of America that would cash it. There was a man in Christian's trailer park I was introduced to through Mark from my mom's RV. Park named Dale. I had gotten a ride from him, but he kept trying to get me to have sex with him, but I wouldn't participate in that behavior any longer. He was so frustrated with me. He straight told me, "Shanon, we all just want you to suck our dicks. If you would just suck our dicks, your life would be better, and all your problems' will go away." I could not believe what I was hearing. I told Dale, 'Please don't ever say that to another women again in your life." I felt strange when he said "we". He was talking about his cult. A cult of satanic murderous men who only wanted to use me and abuse me, and if I didn't follow along with their wants, I was going to continue to be tortured in all aspects of my life.

I received my. Settlement check for my sexual harassment settlement. I had taken Dale out to eat and had him drop me off at the train station. I got on it, and we headed to Santa Ana. I was gonna go to Huntington Beach and get baptized in the water. They were having a church. That was doing statewide baptisms. But when the day came, I didn't want to go because I didn't want to do it in front of everybody, for everybody to watch like a show, because I felt my connection with God was something that was between him and me, and it wasn't meant for the world to see. So I changed my mind. I had already been baptized in prison, and I knew that was valid. When I arrived in Santa Ana, a stranger came up to me and asked me, is it OK for me to talk to you? I don't want your people to get mad at me. I thought that was kind of an odd conversation, but it is what it is. I stayed in Santa Ana for about a month, but I had to go back to Modesto for court. So, I found an Airbnb in Modesto. I made a reservation, got back on another train and headed back to Modesto. I stayed the night at the Airbnb. I woke up promptly and very early, ready and prepared for court. I then got on my phone and. Contacted Lyft. My Lyft account was not working. I assumed maybe I didn't have money ,for it, so I went over to the store quickly. I put $200.00 in my account. I got back on the app,, and it is still not working. I didn't know what to do. I had no one to call. So I got on Uber, and I made an Uber app a profile. I then tried that, but it didn't work either. So then I called a taxi service. The taxi service never showed up either. At this point, it was 20 minutes after court. I knew I was going to have a warrant. My bill was $250,000, and it was going to be raised, and I was going to be arrested. I found a stranger that said he would give me a ride. He got me there in about 10 minutes. So, I was about 30 minutes late to court. Usually, when I went to court, I was there till around noon because I would always be the last one called this particular day. I was the first one called. The court was closed, and they were starting a trial. The bailiff told me to come up to the clerk's office and get back on the docket. So, I filed my docket. The hearing went to the bail office, and the proof of this was obtained. And was waiting over the weekend, which was Memorial weekend, for the judge to approve a new hearing date. I knew the date would be set out for a few months, so I got on a train and headed to Santa Cruz. I arrived in Santa Cruz and got a hotel. And then I was treated like a common horror by the owner. He asked me to suck his cock. I explained to him that I didn't do that and went about my day. As I came back to the hotel, I saw five cop cars in the hotel's driveway. That's when I knew something was wrong. I immediately understood that I should not go back to the hotel because I knew they were waiting for me. I stayed away until around 1:00 in the morning. When I came back to the hotel, I couldn't get into my room, so I slid the window open and climbed in. I put on my pajamas and laid on the bed. There was a bang on the door, and it was the police. I had not locked the door with the bolt and knew they were just gonna come in. And that's exactly what they did. They came in they arrested me for a warrant because I was waiting for the judge to approve the hearing date. I was then arrested and spent five days in Santa Cruz jail. While in this jail, I met a woman who told me I was the truth. She told me how she told God she would give me my money back and that every time she walked down the street, something would shove their finger or something up her rear. She said it was so hard and deep into her bottom it would hurt her physically. I could tell she was scared by the look on her face. Something was haunting her that she couldn't see. Karma was getting her, and she knew I was the reason why. This other woman told me I was the truth too! It is so crazy when people you don't know are telling you things about your self in a manner from the spirit realm. I knew all the things I had been through were real,, and people were paying for them all over the place, which I did not even know. I knew that what was going on was way bigger than me.

When Santa Stanislaus County came and picked me up. The officer who came and picked me up was very kind and considerate, and I told him the situation in my story as we went on our drive back to Modesto. When we arrived in Modesto, he had to take my things because I didn't have them. They didn't have enough room for my stuff in the facility. I had to pick and choose what I was taking. I was gonna put my Bible in my backpack and have him hold it when he reminded me, wait, you might need that when you get out. And I said, ohh, you're right. So I had him put it with my things, and I was so glad that I did that because that is what I need :my Bible is the true thing. It's what I go to. God is number one in my life, and when I got out of jail, I needed to praise Him for all he has done for me.

I was put into a cell around 4:00 in the morning. I was completely exhausted when the door opened. The officer asked if I was OK, and I said I was hungry. I haven't eaten all day once since I got transferred here. She said a good thing, here's breakfast. I was served breakfast. I ate. I slept. And the next day, I realized there was a woman there that I'd known from the Tuolumne County Jail from my first arrest before I went to prison. Harley Price check. Harley Price Check is a very kind person,, and she has been in there for three years, waiting on her trial. She helped me in any manner that she could, which brought joy to my heart. She had a few books in her cell, and she let me read them. Uh, one in particular book was called The Epic of Humanity. As I read this book, I realized that Harley knew exactly what I was going through because she knew about the things that were in the book. This book was about the Annunaki and about ancient civilizations, and secret societies. This led me to believe why Harley and I were so connected from the beginning when I met her the first time. I spent a few days alone in the cell, and then I was given a cellmate. My cellmate came in, and I said hi, Bunky. This woman was on fentanyl. She was filthy and dirty, and she smelled. I felt really bad for her and tried to do everything to comfort her as she came into the room. I gave her the bottom bunk because she was falling off of the bed because she was high on fentanyl. She began to write a note. And her. Intoxicated state. And I was concerned as to. Her health. And her state of mind. And I told her she should probably lie down and rest. And I took the paper and paid pencil from her. I told her we have to keep our minds protected from the enemy, and her statement was who's the enemy? I began to explain to her how the devil works in our lives and how he destroys it, and she pretended that she didn't know anything about what I was talking about. The next day. She became irate and was very rude to me, so I asked her to please move off of my bed. She wouldn't move, so I pulled her mattress onto the floor. She was very ill, so she didn't fight too much about that, but she climbed onto her back mattress. And laid on the floor. She turned her back to me and was facing the wall and began masturbating. I couldn't believe my eyes as to what I was seeing. She was licking her fingers, and then she looked back at me and said what? I didn't respond, and I just continued to read my Bible. As I was reading the

Bible, this woman started speaking in a demonic voice. She said. You know God's doing this to you, don't you, you stupid ditch." You're the devil's wife, and you're God's daughter," and "He did more to you than he did to Jesus." And then my cell mate's voice would come out normal, and she would say," Help me bunky, it's not me, help me Bunky. And then the demon would come back, and he told me if you keep. Getting that Bible. I'm gonna hurt this one. I never responded verbally. But I knew I had authority over this demon. So I asked it what its name was. He replied. I am Beelzebub. And continue to masturbate. I got the attention of one of the officers as he went by to do checks. I alerted him to this woman's demonic behavior, and he opened the cell door. The officer told me, "if you can't get along, I am going to pull you both out and hand-cuff you and put you in the cold room. I had no idea what the cold room was like, but it did not sound good. I continued to read my bible, and this woman finally went to sleep. The next morning. They called her to go to medical while she was out of the cell. I found the note she had started writing when she came into my cell the first night. I could not believe my eyes when I read what she wrote. It was a love poem from Beelzebub to me. It went like this.

Some people say, my love
Can not be true
Please, believe me, my love
And I will show you
I will give you those things

217

You thought unreal
The sun, the moon, the stars,
All bear my seal

This was a poem a demon wrote to me. I knew it was from the devil because the demon Beelzebub had told me I was the devil's wife. This really freaked me out. I could not stay in this cell with this demon another day. I was yelling out of the speaker area to the officers." Get Me Out of this room. Shame on you. How do you sleep at night? Please move me. I can't be with this lady in this room." An officer eventually came and moved me to a room down the hall. That morning at 3:00 AM, three or 4 is when they serve breakfast. I heard a loud bang on the ground, and I thought they dropped the trays with the food on them. I asked my new cellmate to go look and see what it was. To her surprise, she said, Ohh, my goodness, somebody jumped off the tear. I immediately sprung off of my bed and ran over to the door. I peered out the little tiny window to witness my old cellmate was splattered on the ground. She had jumped off the top tier. Her head was cracked open, and there was blood everywhere. Her face had started to swell. I almost couldn't recognize her. It was the most horrific thing I'd ever seen in my life. All the officers came running in to assist, as did the fire department. I was trembling and shaking. It made me think back to when Beelzebub had said, "If you keep reading that bible, I am going to hurt this one." I had been reading my Bible in my new room when it happened. She had jumped right in front of my new room. As if the devil wanted me to see that he did, in fact, follow through with hurting her. There were four other suicide attempts in 25 days. I knew the devil was at work in the jail. He couldn't get me, so he was trying to take other women. I had gone to court with one of the girls who tried to kill herself. The other women had been making fun of her on the bus on the way to court, and she denied that she had tried to hurt herself. I looked at her tattoos and saw the Illuminati sign on her wrist. I grabbed her hand ,turned her arm over, and asked her why she got the tattoo and if she was part of them. She said yes, but she did not know what the sign meant. I leaned in and told her I knew she tried to kill herself and told her not to ever try that again. I also told her to turn from that group and look to God. He will change your life. He will help you if you ask Him. She put her head down in shame but looked up at me with sadness in her eyes and shook her head in agreement with me. I felt glad that I had gotten a chance to speak with her. At court this day, I was telling the girls about my family being a part of the illuminati and how Dale had told me if I would just suck all their dicks, I would not have all these problems. A lady kind of made of a joke and said your family's part of a dick-sucking cult! And I said yes, it is a dick-sucking cult. Lol. And we all laughed about it. But in reality, it is not funny. It's true, though. One of the women spoke up and said she was being gang stalked too and was in jail for being harassed at the Dollar General store. I related to her story because I was arrested falsely at the 99-cent store. I sat right next to her and told her we were going to get these people. I also told her how to deal with them by not reacting to their harassment. I wanted to help her conquer the demons that were attacking her, too. She also told me how strange it was that her mother showed up to court because they were not close. I explained to her that our families are involved in our destruction. I on the way back from court, I was placed in an area of the bus with another woman. It was just her and I. She asked me why I was in jail, so I told her the truth. I explained all the torment I had been through. She told me she believed in me and said I should write a book. I told her I would love to start my book, but I had no money on my books to buy any paper or pencils. I felt so happy after spreading the word of my story that day to all these women, and for this one lay to tell me she believed in me was amazing. That evening, one of the jail workers came by my room, and I saw a yellow notepad slide under my door. It had a note on it that said I believe in you, and I believe in your story. Here is a notepad to start your book. It was from the woman on the bus. I broke down crying and was so excited to be able to start this book. I looked out across the jail up at her room, and she was standing in the window. I held my hands up in the shape of a heart to express my thanks and love for her help. She blew a kiss at me and threw up the same sign with her hands. I immediately went to the desk in my cell and began to write. I wrote her a note back that thanked her for her belief in me and told her I was going to dedicate my book to her. She was the catalyst for my future and for getting me on my true path of exposing them in a worldwide manner without being blocked by this cult. They can't stop me from being creative and writing my truth, and they can't stop me from publishing this book, either. I was so jazzed up that I had met a woman who was all about helping my cause. Which was something they couldn't take away from me.

The next day, for the 3rd time, the mental nurses came to my cell. I was frustrated that they kept coming to my cell. The usual protocol for them to come to your cell is put in a request form after the initial questioning when you first come into the facility. I told them, "Go away, I am fine". This time, the Sergeant was with the nurses. The Sergeant asked me if he "can I ask you a few questions." I had no problem answering his questions. He asked me, "What do you have to live for."? I replied," God is who I live for"! He then asked me, "How do you deal with making it in here."? I replied once again," God, "and pointed my finger to heaven. He looked agitated with me and shut the cell door. Now, mind you, this place had me locked down 60 hours at a time. Only to be let out for 3 hr. to shower, make phone calls and exercise. I had been calling my father for days with no answer. My grand-mother finally answered but was rude and said she had nurses at her home and was embarrassed by me calling from the jail. Not to call but to write to her. I wrote her a letter and asked her some questions I had always had since I was a kid. She was writing back to me back but had no answers to my questions, no support or concern for my wellbeing. I only worried about what I was making her look like. Even though I was innocent of the charges she kept saying in her letters she tried putting money on my books but was unable to because the website was not working, but I knew that was not true because everybody else in the jail had money on their books with no problems.

My new cellmate and I had been getting along pretty well. A few days had gone by, and she was getting out soon. I knew Harley. And Harley was pretty cool with the police officers. So, one day at Wreck, one of the officers called me over to her desk and asked if I wanted to be on the top bunk. And I said not really. And she said well, I'm moving you to the bottom bunk permanently, would you like that? And I said yes. Harley and her friends had said you could thank us for that. I was so blown away by the utter respect that I was getting while in jail because nobody wanted to be on the top of it. But I'm not the type of person to argue or fight with people over such petty things. That night, because the girl had been moved to the top, she was in a bad mood, and she was throwing a fit. She started talking crap about God and saying your God doesn't put people in jail. Explain that to me. I told her, I guess you haven't read the Bible because people do go to jail in the Bible. Sometimes you have to. He saves you by putting you in jail. I wasn't gonna go too much further in it because she said. What are you gonna do now about me? I said I'm not gonna do anything, and I'm just gonna pray to God. About 10 minutes later, an officer came and opened the door and asked her to step out. I didn't know what was going on because it wasn't none of my business anyway. She left the room. She was gone for about 10 minutes. The officer came back and told me to start packing her things because she was moving. I gladly jumped up on her bunk, started packing her things and handed them to the officer. The whole time, I was thinking, wow, God, you showed this one. Don't talk about him because he's going to prove you wrong every time. Instant karma. She had been moved within 10 minutes of her talking crap about him. I watched her walk up the stairs to her new room, and she looked over at me in shock, her mouth wide open, as if she didn't understand how this had happened. Previously, when she was throwing her fit, she had been saying I'm gonna move you out of my room, this is my room. I had this room 1st, and that's when the officer opened the door, and she got moved. I said God, thank you for moving her. Thank you for hearing me and showing her who the boss is. I had met another woman in jail named Laura. She had said she was a chosen one, and her birthday was 7/7/77. God's numbers. I was quick to believe her until she pulled me aside and began to tell me a story about how she was part of the cult. She told me she was with them one night and that the cult had taken a little baby down to the river and slit its throat. When the blood from the baby hit the water, the water began to swirl around in a circle with the blood. I stopped her instantly from going on with her story and told her I didn't want to hear anymore and plugged my ears. I asked her what she was doing with this cult and why she joined. She said, "It was my sister"! I did not like her answer because we all have choices, and she chose wrong. I walked away from her and decided I was not going to talk to her ever again. After that day, I ignored her.

This other woman came into the jail. She had been in the room I was in when I had been falsely arrested the first time years before. I remembered her face and how mean she was to me then. I had planned on not speaking to her, but one day during rac, she asked me how I was doing and called me by name. It was confusing for me because I did not know this woman. I responded to her questions and was confident with her. She then told me how she knew my sister Cassie, and how she was very, very nice to me. She had told me how my sister had come into the jail 3 days after I had bailed out years before. She also told me my sister had sold one of her babies to another woman who was in jail with them, and she was demanding the woman put money on her books for commissary for payment due for the baby. I learned my sister had been selling the babies she was pregnant with to this cult. I was so hurt to know this horrific information about my own family. I thought, how could my sister be so evil? I was finally getting the full circle of the story. The woman had also told me her man and 2 year old child had died. Her man got sick and died. Then, her daughter had died in her sleep. Within two weeks, she had lost her entire family. Knowing this women was part of what happened to me, I knew what had happened to her was God and Karma. She sure seemed to be a nicer person to me this time and was definitely not the same person I had been around years before. I could tell she had been humbled. I could see she knew she had been a part of something that had ruined her life.

I spent three months in jail. I didn't know what was gonna happen because I had so many cases built up against me. I was looking at 25 to life. They had lied about me having strikes, and I didn't know what was going to happen. I just left it up to God. I had gotten a public defender, and she had told me to just trust the process. At this point in my life, I didn't trust anybody, and I still wanted to try to get the lawyer that I had paid. He never would return my calls, and he took the money and never. Represented me. At the end of the court process, I want it with the public defender. I walked into court, not expecting to go home. I came around the corner, and she asked me do you want to go home today? And I said yes. I ended up being charged with petty theft, even though none of my charges were concerning theft. I couldn't quite understand that, but I took it, and I took it in stride. I was trusting the process. I went back to the jail that night. And I had announced to all the girls that I had met I'm going home, and they were so happy for me. I had met quite a few women in there that I had shared the word with and tried to give positive, uplifting words to. One in particular I ran across was a girl named Lisa. Lisa was part of the cult. Her boyfriend was trying to bring her in on it. She said she was on the fence and wasn't sure which side she was going to take. She knew about gang stalking, she knew about harassment, and she knew about me. She had told me they were all scared. They all went underground. They're all hiding. Lisa seemed to truly want to find the Lord, and I would give her verses to look up and ways to get closer to God. I met a girl at court that day, and she was getting out that night, too. She told me her man could give me a ride out of the jail. Which was great for me because I have nobody to call to pick me up and the jail is really far out in the country. As we left the jail, I was so glad to never look back at it because I don't plan on ever being a part of that scene again. We climbed into her boyfriend's truck, and I felt so much relief as we drove off. I stuck my hand out the window in a waving form to fill the breeze blowing on my face and my arm in freedom. I had them drop me off at Mikes's house. Because I had talked to Mike prior. From the jail. He had told me I could go to his house even though he was on vacation. I got to his house, and I wanted to take a hot bath, soak, relax, and enjoy the fact that I was no longer imprisoned. I stayed the night at Mikes. He had assumed that he would be back the next day. I didn't have a phone to call him. All of a sudden, I heard the garage door open at his house, and I thought it was him. I quietly sat on his couch. Waiting for him. All of a sudden. His. My girlfriend walks into the house that I had never met. She threw a fit, asked me who I was and demanded that I leave. I immediately grabbed my things and told her Mike was just doing a nice thing for me. This has nothing to do with sex. I'm not being with him;, and he's just being a friend to me because I have nowhere to go. She told me she didn't care if she just wanted me to leave. I had nowhere to go. I didn't know what I was going to do. And I was waiting for Mike to come back to take me to the bank to cash the check that the jail had given me back from the cash I had when I was arrested. I walked away and found my way to the bank, cashed the check, and hopped on the train. I headed to LA. I stayed in LA for about a week, and of course, they were harassing me there as well. My intuition had told me they were up to something. I needed to leave L.A. at the airport. Las Vegas was the soonest flight out of town, so I headed there. I figured since these creatures were no longer laughing and things were serious. God had to be down here taking care of things with his own hands. Vegas is full of demons, so I thought what a better place to go to slay some more demons than Vegas. When I was in Las Vegas, I met a strange man who told me they missed me and hugged me. I was creeped out. I couldn't stand being in Vegas. There were so many demons, so much strife, so many blockages, and I could just feel the bad energy there. While I was checking into the Circus Circus Hotel, I was being pushed to the back of the line and was not getting any service. While standing in line when I made eye contact with this man who had demon contact lenses on and black hair. His shirt even said Lucifer on it. He tried to flirt with me and asked me, 'How are you doing'? I replied, "Better than you, Lucifer". He stepped back and was offended by my statement. He said," yes, I am ,Lucifer and I was raised by nuns." Then he said to his friend, "Oh she's a Christian, but look at her judging me". I turned my back on him, but as he walked away, he started laughing at me and said, "Good luck at the end of the line." That's when I said very loud and proud to him, " I may be last right now, But I will be first in the end when it really matters" and laughed out loud for everyone to hear. I could feel the tension in the room coming from everyone that just heard this battle of forces that was being fought in the physical world right in front of them all. I left the next day, got on another plane, and went to Portland, OR. I don't know why I chose Portland, OR. I had never been there. I just thought I would try it out. When I got there, I had been talking to the front desk clerk about regular life. That's when he said, "We can't figure out what you are". Another guest I had met at breakfast one morning had told me about a place called The Grotto. It's a Catholic Church, so beautiful. They also have a church that their congregation would gather in for Catholic services. I went on a walk through the Grotto and recorded the glorious sight. It touched my heart as I walked through the statues of Jesus being crucified and of his betrayals. I was so touched by this sacred place that it brought tears to my eyes. I was very emotional as I walked through the paths of trees and statues placed on this property.

I recorded this wonderous sight and put it on my YOUTUBE even though my platform has been blocked by this cult. They would make sure no one sees my content then and to this day, ensuring no one could hear my messages of how good God is to me and so I can't make any money. Without subscribers or viewers, how can you get monetized right! I didn't really like the vibe in Organ, it was dirty, and it was depressing. I really was just trying to see if I could catch people following me around these different places. I got on a plane, and I headed back to Santa Cruz. The first week back, I was walking to the library when a drunk man came up to me and hugged me. He began to beg for my forgiveness and told me he did not mean to have sex with a little girl. He said his mother made him have sex with a child in front of her for alcohol. He said she would buy him alcohol if he would sexually assault this little girl. I pushed him away and told him, "Go to God, I can't help you." He started crying and was saying he was sorry over and over again. I walked away in horror as to what he had shared with me. It was as if I could give me forgiveness. I could not help such a sick individual. When I walked back, he was passed out on the corner, laying on the sidewalk. In Santa Cruz, at least I knew what was there, and I did have a PO Box there. I felt like I needed some kind of stability even though I had no home. I also had the library to work on this book and focus on getting over what had been happening to me. I am healing by writing this book. I am getting over the traumas these people tried to inflict upon me. Santa Cruz is by the beach, and I feel close to God here. I can grow in his words and form a closer relationship with him. I know he is going to restore all the enemy has stolen, and I will reap a harvest of fruit. I worked on sewing good fruits of the spirit since finding God. I grew in patience, self-control, endurance, long suffering, and I grew in the knowledge that God is, in fact, real. I believe I made believers out of these Satan worshippers. I was God's proof. I stand firm in my story and my testimony I tell you in this book. They crafted a web of complexity, but I walked through it untouched, with God's strength and guidance. In the midst of the chaos, I only gained clarity. Causing me to step out of the darkness into the light and reclaim my soul. I took my personal apocalypse and began to earn my spiritual stripes and ranked up in the army of God. I took the rejection and made it my protection. I wrestled it, twisted it, strangled it by the neck. They made it mine. They thought they were the masters of every move in my life. But I learned life's obstacles are merely steppingstones for those who dare to confront them. So, I wore a smile and held my head high while they played games. I changed the rules. I mastered my fears. And stood unbreakable in the game they thought they had already won. God had allowed me to see them, which made them retreat from my light. You have to keep going no matter what. Each scar, every wound, was how I faced it head-on, refusing to back down. No one could take the strength that I earned with my own blood and strength transformed. Thrive and strive to become that force of unstoppable will. I am turning the end of all things into the beginning of my legacy. They turned their serenity into a weapon and used words as an aspect of currency, their words and tears to become a Boom. a form of manipulation that is hard to escape. They made the rules of engagement. There are only theirs to write. They tried to become my nightmare, but I became the nightmare they could not shut out. I did not need to lift a finger or make a move. I simply left it up to the Highest in every battle they tried to throw at me. The truth is the raw, untamed force that they would rather die than face. Just thought I was still here and alive. It keeps the colt looking over their shoulders in fear of the unescapable karma. Peace was something I stole the moment they met me. I wanted to become something to them that wouldn't die but something that wouldn't linger in their lives. Betrayal cuts deep, but my courage in this aftermath cuts deeper. My courage does not come from anger. For revenge, but from an unshakable resilience and a silent but powerful defiance to stay true to myself. This defiance will haunt those who thought they could break me. When someone betrays you, they expect you to react, to be shattered, to be enraged. They were prepared for explosions, ready to revel in my pain, hoping they'd left a mark. Instead, I rise with a calmness and a strength that doesn't seek validation. I didn't need to prove it to anyone. I chose peace over chaos. This is louder than any shout, louder than any argument. I refuse to let their betrayal define me. I chose to have something they'll never have. My courage and my dignity. I didn't sink to their level. I did not let their actions strip away my dignity and my self-worth. It's a bitter pill. They tried to shatter me but only left me. Left there in their own brokenness, my courage, a mirror showing them the truth of everything they'll never be. My courage is testament. Who I really AM, and that is a child of God. I turned their betrayal into something that strengthened me. I won the battle, and I never knew I was fighting. And that is the battle for our souls in the unseen realms. So, my greatest revenge is living well. They did not realize God was there in my darkest moments, turning my pain into purpose. When everyone else walked away, God stayed. People didn't want to accept me. I had to accept myself. You have to earn yearn for something more. That's when the spark ignites. The world isn't here to celebrate uniqueness, and it's here to crush it. And with the power of God, I turn every moment intended to break me into something better, clearing a path for an entirely new and righteous path that He has intended for me. There is no higher purpose than to see what you're made of. This is my purpose, and no one could take it away. I have become stronger, faster, better and more resilient in the face of the wicked community that tried to keep me small and hidden from the world if I would conform to what they. Thought I would be dead right now. Today, I am no longer bound by the limits they tried to put on me. People don't even realize you're trapped in a cage. A mental cage. Every fire only strengthens the steel within, the steel of the sword of the spirit that cuts off the lies of the deception they had placed. In my view, the truth became a double-edged sword. This journey filled with pain was only the catalyst that launched me into purpose. God had intended for me. I am living proof that strength comes from something within and not from external circumstances. This has brought me to a place of unshakeable faith and true purpose. I don't back down. I don't fold under pressure. I lean into it. I unleash the monster inside of me. All they did was sharpen the claws of the monster within. It's not about vengeance, and it's about victory. My monster found strength within. There, within. There was none left. They wanted me to stay in the lane and play by their rules the. The hunger inside to not be mediocre became my driving force. I refused to settle for less than what I deserved. The moment you push me too far is the moment you'll regret it. Because once the monster in me is awake, the obstacles and the laughs seem to see fear as a way to grow and evolve into something they can never be. I've been pushed to the limit and instead of breaking, I was turned into a diamond. The monster inside of me is real, and it's here to win. I have been through the fire. And walked through the storms. And all because of my faith in the promises that God has for me. My faith in a monster seed is the monster they now fear. I had the key and unlocked every door they didn't even know existed. Elevated by my newfound self-worth and the resilience I'd cultivated, I refused to live my life. With their agenda, they can't undo the fire they helped ignite. They thought when I was down, I was down for the count. But now all. I was just awakened. They thought my silent strength was a sign of submission. But the spirit inside of me was stronger than any fear they could conjure. He is stronger inside of me than he who is living in the world. This is my story, written in the ink of Resilience. There is a battle going on, whether you realize it or not, a battle between good and evil, and we are all participants. Willing or not! Today, my life is full of peace and calm. I no longer have these people stalking me or bothering me. God had granted me a rebirth. I have been made new and transformed by the renewing of my mind. The old has gone, and the new is here. What is going on in my life is a divine transformation. I am waiting on the Lord's timing and trusting that he has a plan for me. He has a plan for my highest potential, and I am ready for this transformation. I am sure I will be writing another book about my transformation in the future so you all can read about the glorious life he is getting ready to give me. I hope that my story has brought some enlightenment to you and a new way to think about the lives we live. We are more than this physical world. We are spirits having a human experience. Embrace the struggles God puts in your path because in the struggle, you will find the path that you were meant to be on. He will lead you if you allow Him to. I knew God would not leave me for my sake and my story proves that God is real and He will help you if you trust the process and trust that the universe has something better for you. Better than any of the worldly things we are taught to hold on to. He who lives in me is greater than he who is in the world.

Photobombed by one of my gang stalkers. 2019

*Columbia National Park in Columbia CA. where my grandmother lives.
The illuminati sign on a building there. 2022*

The light on the building in Columbia,CA. 2022

Spiritual Attachment Guide

*The town entrance sign in Turlock Ca my hometown zoomed
in. 2024*

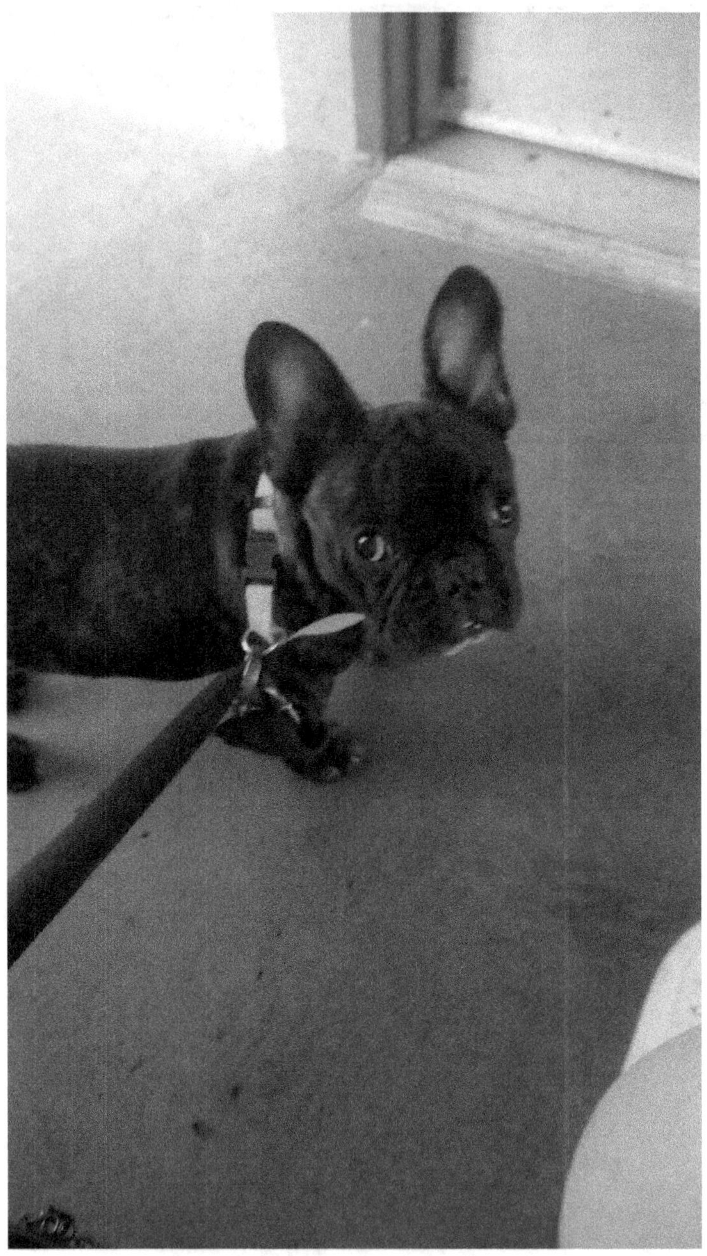

Zander my sweet puppy the cult stole and sacrificed

Photo of my first cat fish from the illuminati

The town entrance sign for Turlock Ca. Full picture. 2024

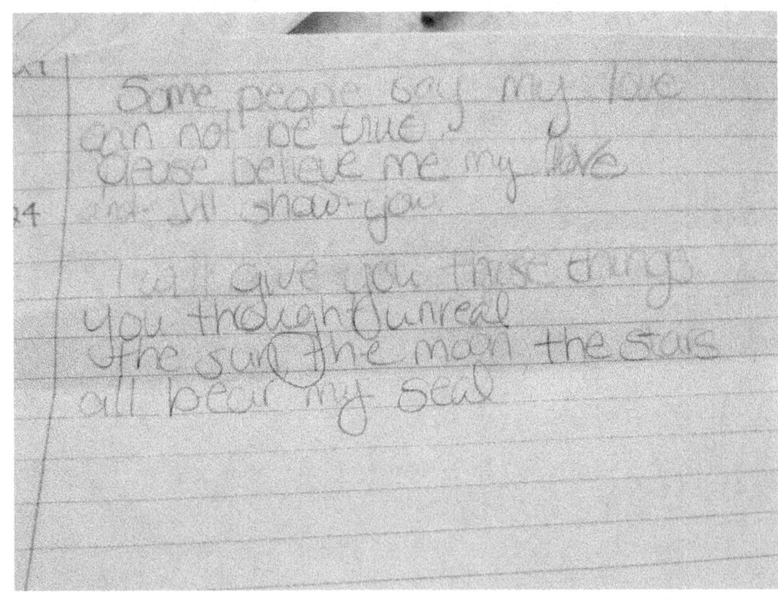

The hand written poem by cellmate possessed by Belezubub.

My mother Joanne and I at Columbia park when I was 6 1983

Marylin was also part of mk Ulta and gang stalking

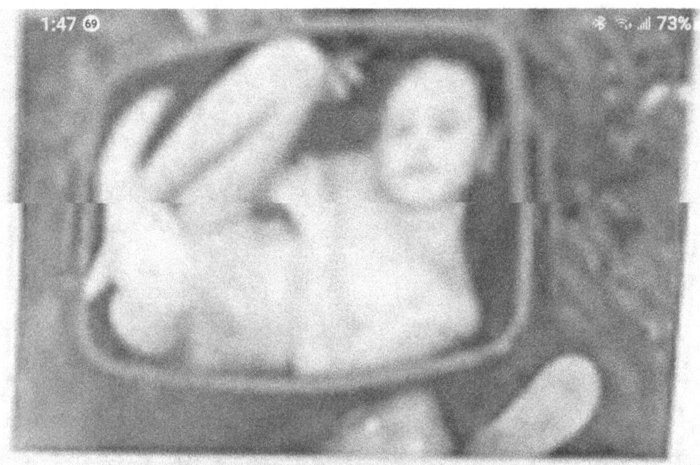

This is a photo from Jaimie Lee Curtis dinning room.

www.ingramcontent.com/pod-product-compliance
Lightning Source LLC
Chambersburg PA
CBHW070751160726
48004CB00001B/146